Madame Wu's Handbook on Home-Cooking

The Song Dynasty Classic on Domestic Cuisine

吳氏中饋錄

Madame Wu's Handbook on Home-Cooking
The Song Dynasty Classic on Domestic Cuisine

吳氏中饋錄

Translated and Annotated by:
Sean J.S. Chen

Forewords by:
Eugene N. Anderson *and* Miranda Brown

Linea

Copyright © 2023 Linea Publishing Inc.

All rights reserved. No part of this publication may be used or reproduced in any manner whatsoever without written permission from the publisher except in the case of brief quotations embodied in critical articles and reviews.

For information or other requests, contact Linea Publishing at: `info.linea@protonmail.com`

First edition, 2023

Library and Archives Canada Cataloguing in Publication

Title: Madame Wu's handbook on home-cooking : the Song Dynasty classic on domestic cuisine / translated and annotated by Sean J.S. Chen ; forewords by Eugene N. Anderson and Miranda Brown.
Other titles: Wushi zhongkuilu. English
Names: Madame Wu, active 13th century, author. | Chen, Sean Jy-Shyang, translator, annotator. | Anderson, E. N. (Eugene Newton), Jr., 1941- writer of foreword. | Brown, Miranda, 1975- writer of foreword.
Description: First edition. | Translation of: Wushi zhongkuilu. | Includes bibliographical references and index. | Includes some text in Chinese.
Identifiers: Canadiana (print) 20230577962 | Canadiana (ebook) 20230577970 | ISBN 9781777938727 (hardcover) | ISBN 9781777938710 (softcover) | ISBN 9781777938703 (PDF)
Subjects: LCSH: Cooking, Chinese—Early works to 1800. | LCSH: Cooking, Medieval—China—Early works to 1800. | LCSH: Cooking—China—History—To 1500. | LCGFT: Cookbooks.
Classification: LCC TX724.5.C5 W8713 2023 | DDC 641.5951—dc23

ORIGINAL AUTHOR: Anonymous Song dynasty author known as Madame Wu (吳氏)

PRIMARY SOURCE: 陶宗儀 (編), 陶珽重 (輯). "說郛". 九十五. 1646. Harvard Yenching Library (FHCL.YENCH). Harvard University. https://nrs.harvard.edu/urn-3:FHCL:22928922

ACADEMIC REVIEWERS: Eugene N. Anderson & Miranda Brown

REVISION: 32ee968

Published by Linea Publishing Inc.
Toronto, Ontario, Canada

FOREWORD

By Eugene N. Anderson

"*Madame Wu's Record of Provisions*" 吳氏中饋錄 is one of the earliest Chinese cookbooks. H. T. Huang writes:

> Tradition has it that this is the work of a Madame Wu of Kiangsu who lived during the Sung dynasty. It first appeared in *Shuo Fu* 說郛, the collection published by Thao Tsung-I [Tao Zongyi] of the Yuan... [N]oteworthy as the first Chinese cookbook in which exact measurements are given..." (Huang, 2000, p.127).

It probably reflects the cooking of well-to-do but not rich or powerful families: local landed gentry, literati without national power, small-scale to medium-scale merchants. The pattern of foodstuffs reflects a lower Yangtze pattern, making Madame Wu's alleged Jiangsu origin quite believable. Fish, shellfish, and a wealth of greens dominate. Pork is the only meat specified. Frequent use of red ferment seems to point toward Fujian, but red molds were apparently more widely used in the past than they are now. Even today, Carolyn Phillips' encyclopedic cookbook [18] records them in many places well beyond the Fujian stronghold.

Madame Wu was writing in a realm where wheat and rice were staples, though millets retained a strong presence. Pork was the main meat, but lamb and beef were important in the north and northwest. Dairy products, limited to butter in Madame Wu's book, were staples in those areas. The famous fast-growing, high-yield rice varieties from Champa [11] had probably come, but were barely known; Madame Wu probably never heard of them. Soybeans had taken their strong lead as source of sauces, ferments, and pastes. soy-sauce making was a new art, and Madame Wu was aware of it. Ordinary people in areas like Jiangsu lived on rice, small fish, and vegetables, with occasional meat and sweets, and this is the cuisine Madame Wu recorded.

The book reflects a cooking tradition developing into a sophisticated cuisine, but not fully there yet. As several have pointed out since Michael Freeman's classic monograph on Song food [11], China's cuisine, simple through the Tang dynasty, took a leap in Song toward true self-conscious gourmet style. Jack Goody showed in his important book *Cooking, Cuisine and Class* [12] that elaborated cuisines generally require a middle class to develop. A two-class society consists of a vast mass who eat the staple food and a few vegetables, and an elite that gorges on meat and expensive ingredients but does little with them. This is a fairly accurate description of Tang food, though some Central Asian elaborations had appeared. In Song, a middle-class cuisine evolved, and this is reflected in Madame Wu's recipes. They are for people who have considerably more than mere staples, but are not able to live on the "meat and alcohol" traditionally equated with luxury in Chinese writings.

Chinese cuisine, in this sense of a self-consciously elaborated tradition, evolved in large part from the needs to preserve food. Already in the Han dynasty there were many recognized ways to save food: pickling, fermenting, drying, smoking, cooking till dry and hard, and packing in protective materials ranging from oil to sugar. Food could even be mixed with pesticides; grain was saved by mixing it with powerfully insecticidal powdered Artemisia and sieving out the poisonous powder before using the grain as food [9, p.29]). The great work *Qimin Yaoshu* by Jia Sixie has long and detailed sections on all these methods [16][13].

H.T. Huang's detailed monograph on Chinese food preservation [13] records the full history of this art, which is probably the most elaborate in the world. Madame Wu's cookbook is a perfect example of the midpoint of this tradition, when it was developing from the rustic world of Jia toward the sophisticated, refined gourmetship of later writers. Yuan Mei's *Recipes from the Garden of Contentment* [8], also ably translated by Sean Chen, has relatively few such recipes, and they are of a more complex and subtle order. Madame Wu was deeply involved in preserving food. At least 51 of the 80-odd recipes in the book are for foods to keep. In a few cases she warns us that a recipe for preserved vegetables "...is not for those in a rush to eat them..." (See Page 42; there are 75 entries in the book, but several include more than one recipe). Most of what is preserved is vegetables, including rustic and humble ones like cucumbers, again reflecting a society of small landowners and householders.

Near contemporary with Madame Wu is a cookbook by the great artist Ni Zan [1]. He was writing in Yuan, but the food world he records is that of Song, from the same lower Yangtze region. It has none of the Central Asian influences that appeared during Yuan. He too has many recipes for preserved food, as well as for brewing and fermentation. Moreover, since like many another artist before and since, he faced some lean times, his book reflects a similarly middle-class reality. Luxuries were few. Like earlier writers, he apparently brewed his own ale, though his brewing recipes are corrupted and hard to follow.

Forward-looking recipes in Madame Wu include the one for slippery water noodles (See Page 88); its complex and subtle flavoring, including sesame butter and many spices, recalls Yuan dynasty cuisine as reflected in the *Yinshan Zhengyao* and other books [6].

Perhaps Tang dynasty cuisine already had such foods, but we have no record of them. Such gourmetship appears to be largely a Song development.

Another significant point is the presence of Central Asian baked goods. A compact group of six recipes, for halva, shortbread, and samosas, represents the western tradition. There is even one recipe called by a much-attenuated western name, *saboni*. As Sean Chen points out, this is from the Turkic word *sabuniye*. That comes from Arabic sabuniyah "soapy", which in turn is from Greek *sapouni*, "soap". Central Asian baking and baked goods had been influential since Han and especially since the Northern and Southern Dynasties. These sweets were to continue in popularity, as seen in Guo Lian's late Ming food book [7], and indeed some are still popular, especially in northwest China.

Madame Wu's world is one in which people still brewed their own alcohol, made their own soy-sauce, prepared their own pickles, and lived on small fish, shellfish, and fresh vegetables and grain, with little meat or fruit. It was a local cuisine, using materials available on one's own farm, or at least in one's immediate region. It was a world of thrift, in which every garlic shoot and chive leaf was worth considerable effort in saving for future meals. It was a world of some exciting innovations, from soy-sauce — new at the time — to sesame paste with spiced noodles, and yet a world steeped in tradition, including the time-honored preservation techniques that go back to the days of Fan Shengchi and Jia Sixie.

The flavors await kitchen testing, but from cooking similar items, from shortbread to Yuan variants on the slippery noodle dish, I can testify that many, if not most, of these recipes should produce wonderful results. Madame Wu was a discerning, thoughtful, careful cook, whose innovatively exact measurements show her real skill. Compiling so long and sophisticated a cookbook in Song times took much effort and writing time. The recipes are well worth experimenting. Perhaps a Song-Yuan restaurant is in our future.

Sean Chen rounds out his careful and excellent translation with thorough, interesting notes that identify ingredients, explain terms, speculate on cooking and preparing methods, and indicate important culinary innovations and continuities. We have long needed a translation of this historically important work. We have thousands of translations of the philosophical classics, but almost no translations of ordinary works on the wants and needs of everyday life. Sean Chen is an adventurer into that little-studied literature.

I would love to have met Madame Wu, to talk with her (somehow magically absorbing rural Song dialect), find out about her life, find out why she wrote down a unique and innovative cookbook. I think of her as rather like my grandmother, who could not rest until our cabinets were filled with jams, jellies, and preserves for the winter. Did Madame Wu's friends and neighbors implore her to save her skills for posterity? Did she need to write instructions for workers? One thing we know: she loved good food.

Foreword

By Miranda Brown

I remember first encountering a seventeenth-century copy of *Cooking Manual* 吳氏中饋錄 in a library in the Fall of 2016. It was a disarmingly slim volume and its contents lacked any sort of literary conceit. That edition composed rows upon rows of recipes, written in a terse idiom — a striking contrast to Yuan Mei's celebrated *Suiyuan Shidan*. But the contents of the Cooking Manual are every bit as rich. The cookbook, one of two surviving food treatises authored by a woman before the twentieth century, offers clues about every day life during the Southern Song dynasty.

We learn, for example, about how home cooks preserved their vegetables and freshly slaughtered meat, the techniques they used to add umami to their meals, and (most strikingly) the Song addiction to sweets. We also learn just how far the foodways of the Middle East permeated life in coastal China. Cooking Manual includes recipes for foods related to Syrian bazarek, halva, and zulabiya (the Persian pastry related to jalebi and churros). These confections provide the clearest evidence of the impact of the Maritime Silk Road, which connected coastal China to ports along the Indian Ocean, on the Chinese diet.

Sean Chen does a terrific job rendering this historical gem into English and providing the necessary historical context. His translation will be a must-read for students of Chinese gastronomy, historians, and undergraduates for generations to come. It provides a wealth of information about cross-cultural culinary exchanges in medieval China — and about the relationship between the cooking of Madame Wu's day and those of the present. And in this way, recovers a lost world of eating that continues to shape the meals of the present.

Translator's Preface

By Sean J.S. Chen

Upon completing the bulk of the work for *Recipes from the Garden of Contentment* (*Suiyuan Shidan*, 隨園食單) in 2018 [8], I started mulling over what I should try doing next in terms of a project. It would be quite an understatement to say that translating the *Suiyuan Shidan* was a rewarding experience. Even while the book was still a translation project on the blog, I was able to participate as an advisor to a documentary that would eventually become a PBS series. The resulting published books a few years later won international awards, among other media mentions. From all this, I met many incredible people along the way and was honestly surprised by the response. Needless to say, I am very much thankful for it all.

Nevertheless, that project was a six-year-long, all-consuming journey, which diverted much quality time I could spend with the family and the desperately needed recuperation from employed work. From these experiences, I resolved that any future translation projects must be more scaled to the realities of daily life. On top of the usual "givens" like choosing a subject that could contribute to the accumulation of knowledge and also piqued my interests, I needed to aim for shorter works that could be completed more quickly using source materials that were readily accessible and of decent quality. Having had to transliterate and cross-reference text from smudged centuries-old first-editions of the *Suiyuan Shidan* from the Harvard and Princeton libraries, I wanted to avoid having a repeat of that experience.

The late Song dynasty manual *Madame Wu's Handbook on Home-Cooking* (*Wushi Zhongkuilu* 吳氏中饋錄) seemed to fit all the criteria. The organization of the work was straightforward and compact. The whole cookbook consisted of a small volume with just three chapters:

- Preserved Meats and Pickled Fish 脯鲊, with 20 recipes
- Preparing Vegetables 制蔬, with 38 recipes
- Sweet foods 甜食, with 15 recipes

It was also included in a Ming dynasty edition of the well-known old Chinese anthology *Shuo Fu* 說郛, and scans of a well-preserved Ming dynasty edition held at the Harvard Yenching Library were readily accessible online.

Most importantly, this book was widely cited as the first published culinary work by a Chinese woman that still existed in its entirety, recording the state of Han Chinese household cuisine from almost eight centuries ago. It was the first work to mention soy-sauce, heralding its gastronomic appearance in Chinese cuisine[17]. Furthermore, other than mentions here and there in various modern academic texts, this would be the first time anyone had translated it to any Western language from Classical Chinese, making its contents and the information more attainable to a broader audience worldwide.

I initially started working on translating the *Wushi Zhongkuilu* due to these straightforward rationales. But as I began reading through Madame Wu's book, it quickly drew me in. With each page I went through, a vastly different culinary landscape revealed itself, and needless to say, I was hooked. From the first recipes, I was presented with a vast array of pickled, dried, and fermented dishes, which points to the sheer importance of cured and preserved foods in domestic cooking and, indeed, the home economics of the time. It seems that one's role in the Song dynasty kitchen was not just to chop ingredients for cooking on the stove but also to marshal over a battalion of curing jars and fermentation vats filled with preserved meats and vegetables so that they could be used when the situation called for it. It was also intriguing that dishes were far more complex in flavouring than expected. While the spices and seasoning utilized would be familiar enough for any modern Chinese chef, most dishes in the cookbook used them in far larger quantities and more surprising combinations. Compared to these dishes from the past, the Chinese cuisine of modern-day Eastern China is relatively simple in seasonings. Hovering between the familiar and the foreign, the recipes and techniques that the cookbook presented were nothing short of captivating.

One thing the reader notices when reading Mandame Wu's cookbook is its utilitarian and unelaborated narration. Although less artistic in delivery than other contemporaneous cookbooks, one gets a sense that the author wrote it for a family to use for preparing their meals. The style and content of the work contrast with the cookbooks and recipes written by the predominantly male authors of the same period, which sometimes feel more like exhibitions of absurd foods. Simply, they look like props for the author's exposition than anything one would wish to consume daily. Yuan Mei referred to this as "Meals for the Ears" 耳餐 and harshly critiqued it, saying: "By boasting the names of expensive and coveted ingredients and flaunting one's wealth to esteemed guests, such meals tease one's ears but confer no satisfaction to one's tongue."[8, p.51] Chinese history scholar H.T. Huang has noted this trend of often grotesque excess and gastronomic exuberances exercised by the male elites during the Song dynasty [13, p.128], which may explain why many of the cookbooks they write, amusing as they are to read, have arguably little practical culinary value. The striking contrast between Madamn Wu's cookbook and that produced by her male contemporaries has also been noticed by Chinese literature scholar Jin Feng, who remarked in her article "The Female Chef and the Nation":

> Rather than discoursing on the transcendental values of food, as male literati did, Mrs. Wu's cookbook provides recipes and practical tips on how to make preserved foods such as pickles, fermented eggs, and fermented tofu. By devoting much space to these pre-prepared foods, it promotes frugality and good housekeeping. (Feng 2016 [10])

Madame Wu's utilitarian work provided detailed proportions of ingredients and instructions for preparing all the dishes it presented, noting when a recipe should or should not be used, all of which should leave little doubt that it was intended for use by one managing the kitchen and cooking for a Medieval Chinese household to be able to reliably recreate each of the listed dishes. The remarkable precision of its recipes, which used standard measurements for much of its ingredients, would have been uncommon for documenting domestic cuisine centuries ago and even to a certain extent in our present times. Indeed, H.T. Huang noted that this work was the first cookbook in Chinese history where exact measurements for ingredients were provided [13, p.127]. All this highlights the role of this cookbook as a manual for transmitting or preserving the culinary knowledge of its author's household.

Things got off to a good start with the project, with more than half of the translations completed by the end of 2019. At that pace, I optimistically planned the completion of the work in less than a year. Then, the new year rolled around, and the spread of a particular virus turned the world upside down. With a pandemic raging onwards, the overt anti-Asian racism and anti-science displays raring its head outside the door, the months-long indoor isolation during lock-down, and overall economic uncertainties, the efforts to complete Madame Wu's Handbook on Homecooking, needless to say, was completely derailed. The process of conducting the translation and research of the book slowed to a crawl, and the encroaching realities of life largely relegated work on the book to the background amidst the blur of numerous more pressing matters. And indeed, there were many.

Still, it was also during this time that I found Madame Wu's cookbook connecting with me. Amids, all manner of social and economic uncertainties happening outside the doors, strangely, I found the unpretentious and matter-of-fact narration of the recipes calming and emotionally grounding.

But then again, it should not be that much of a surprise. After all, being able to create dishes with your bare hands to nourish and lift the spirits of one's family is vastly satisfying, not to mention that few joys in life could parallel preparing one's favourite dishes with one's children and transmitting the recipes to them. And for the ones enjoying the food, what could be more emotionally sustaining than the warm embrace of familiar flavours when we most need it? Imbued with family memories and traditions, they provide an emotional anchor to help us weather uncertainties, providing a source of stability when other aspects of life remain in flux. Perhaps these same feelings and motivation were Madame Wu's *raison d'etre* for writing down these recipes in her cookbook?

Regardless, the recipes and techniques diligently preserved in the writings of Madame Wu now give us one of a few rare snapshots of dinner tables from back during that slice of time in Chinese history. Foods that would have likely been nothing extraordinary or too ordinary at the time now only exist on record because of her desire to note them down for posterity.

Although written centuries before our time, many of the recipes listed in this cookbook would be right at home on the dining tables of many East Asian families, while some others may very well become so with a bit of open-mindedness and coaxing. Even if this was not the case, the aim of Madame Wu's cookbook to leave a legacy and enable her descendants to recreate these cherished dishes is still arguably the same intention for most modern-day family cookbooks, whether handwritten on note cards or published books. Perhaps in the end, despite all the challenges of our work and projects and our daily struggles, despite the glories and accolades we somehow attain, being able to pass on a gift that can help emotionally ground and sustain our descendants is what truly matters.

I want to thank Gene and Miranda for their academic input and keen eyes in proofreading this work's early drafts. I also am deeply indebted to my family for their support in this endeavour, since without their questions, comments, and encouragement, this project (and likely everything else) would have continued to sidetrack into non-existence. Last, I am grateful to Madame Wu for creating the original work and the chain of people throughout history who published it and kept it alive into our modern era. Indeed, it has been a joy to read and a privilege to translate Madame Wu's cookbook, and I hope the readers of this book will derive the same delight and fulfillment I had in getting to know her work.

A Note on Units of Measurement

Near the end of the Southern Song dynasty, when the *Wushi Zhongkuilu* 吳氏中饋錄 was written, weights and measures have long been standardized by the imperial government. However, with the regulatory limitations of the period, variations to the official definitions of various units of measurement existed regionally. On top of this, the amount of time elapsed since the Song dynasty also presents uncertainty to the accuracy of some presently published Song dynasty units of measurement.

Despite that and the fact that dynastic measurements are a subject of continuing research, for the reader's benefit in getting an intuitive grasp of the quantities of ingredients in the recipes, we provide the following Table with the Chinese units mentioned in the cookbook with conversions to Metric units. The values listed are from Tora Yoshida's 1992 work on the period's measurements, which he cautioned as being "...at best approximate." [19]. While they may not be the exact measurements used by Madamn Wu, they would still be usable and helpful as a rough guide in recreating the dishes listed in her cookbook.

Chinese Units	English Translation	Metric Units
Length		
Chi 尺	Chinese foot	31.1 cm
Cun 寸	Chinese inch	3.11 cm
Fen 分		0.311 cm
Volume		
Dou 斗	pint, ladle	6641 mL
Sheng 升	peck	664.1 mL
Ge 合	large cup	66.41 mL
Weight		
Jin 斤	catty, Chinese pound	597 g
Ling 兩	teal, Chinese ounce	37.3 g
Qian 錢	mace	3.7 g

Some non-standard measurements were also used in the work. They include:

Zhan 盞 A small cup with a volume likely around that of a modern Western teacup. The *zhan* was actually used as a unit of time, denoting the amount of time needed for dripping water from a Chinese clepsydra to fill this particular-sized cup, which was around 14.4 minutes.

Gun 滾 An interesting term that simply means "a boil/boiling". Used in this manner, it simultaneously indicates a short period of time in cooking, while also describing the behaviour of the ingredient during the cooking process. In "Recipes from the Garden of Contentment" [8], I calibrated each *gun* to around 3-4 seconds. For measuring somewhat longer periods of cooking time, both incense sticks and graduated candles sticks were used to track time increments of half an hour (刻, ke) up to two hours (時, shi) during the Song and later dynasties. In fact, in some parts of China, this was commonly practiced up to the mid-20th century. For more information on traditional East Asian timekeeping methods, a good starting point (and a thoroughly enjoyable read) is Silvio Bedini's *Scent of Time* [4].

Zhong 鍾 An ancient bronze vessel jar for brewing alcohol and also used as a non-standard unit for volume during the Song dynasty. Finding out the modern metric conversion for this unit is challenging, not least because by Song dynasty almost two millennia had elapsed since the original *zhong* was officially defined, but also because the measurements represented by the units used for its definition had drastically changed. Recorded during the 4th century BCE as "six *hu* and four *dou*" (*luhusidou*, 六斛四斗), various online sources have pinned its metric value as anything between 30 to 200 litres. Even more confusing is that the character "鍾" was sometimes used as a stand-in for "盅" (*zhong*), which is a much smaller non-standard measurement of around half of one *ge* 合, or 33 millilitres. At this point, it suffices to say that the quantity represented by a *zhong* is anyone's guess, or as one of my childhood friends would say: "It's bigger than a bread box.". My take on this is that it is around the size of one of those plastic US gallon milk jugs, which seems like a reasonable volume for the amount of vinegar used in the recipe on Page 33 and the size of the jar's opening on Page 89.

A Note on the Original Title

Considering there is no preface to the work or notes on the author, it should go without saying that information on the *Wushi Shoungkuilu* is quite limited. Indeed, much of what we know about the work and its author could only be inferred from the former's existence in the Ming dynasty edition of the Chinese anthology *Shuofu* 說郛 and its full listed title, namely: "Pujiang Wushi Zhongkuilu" 浦江吳氏中饋錄. As such, dissecting this title into its constituents should be an educational, if not engaging, exercise.

The first part of the title, "*Pujiang*" 浦江, is a city in *Zhejiang* 浙江 province just a few hundred kilometres southwest of Shanghai, which identifies where the work was created and where the author resided. This seems well corroborated by the ingredients in the text bearing the names of regions and cities in Zhejiang, albeit indirectly. In the foreword of "Chinese Gastronomy" [15], the famed bi-lingual writer and translator Lin Yutang claimed that the author lived in "Jiangsu" 江蘇, a province further to the north. Although it is unclear how he determined this, from all the information, we can safely say she lived in China's lush Eastern coastal provinces.

The second part of the title indicates the author as someone of the Wu clan 吳氏. But read in context to the work, *wushi* would mean that the author was a married woman with the *birth surname* Wu 吳. Well before the Song dynasty, using the *shi* 氏 surname identifier typically indicated the birth surname of a married woman, or "maiden name".

The purpose of *shi* has changed in many ways since its first appearance around 1000 BCE in the Bronze Age writings of the earliest cultures of China; nevertheless, the formality, tradition, and prestige it conveys have remained the same. In the stratified societies then, most people would only have a *given name* (*ming*, 名), but those of elite families would have had an ancestral *family name* (*xing*, 姓) on top of their *given name*. This is similar to most cultures' modern use of first and last names. Indeed, the current Chinese term for "full name" combines these two words: *xingming* 姓名. But as power and hierarchy go, those who have amassed more resources or attained more social prestige would necessarily want to differentiate themselves from their numerous cousins of other family branches, and this is where the *clan name* (*shi*, 氏) was used. For example, Confucius, whose family were high officials during the late Shang dynasty, belonged to the clan of *Kong* 孔 of the family *Zi* 子. Using the *clan name* distinguished them from about a dozen other branches with the same *family name*. Still, by the Song dynasty, when Madame Wu completed her cookbook, the differences between the *shi* clan names and the *xing* family names had largely blurred and lost their distinction in common usage.

The third and final part of the name is *zhongkuilu* 中饋錄. While the last character, lu 錄, is easily translated to "records" or "recordings", the first two characters for the word "*zhongkui*" 中饋 are slightly more complicated. Although *zhongkui* could be directly translated as "home-cooking" without a significant loss in accuracy, it is an old term loaded with history and additional meanings that invokes the traditional roles of women in a Chinese family as a wife and the importance of food preparation as part of domestic work. On the matter of *zhongkui*, the 800 BCE *Yi Jing* 易經 (translated in English as "Book of Changes") stated quite pithily in eight characters that: "...by not acting on her compulsions and focusing on her central role in home-cooking a persevering wife will bring good fortune." (無攸遂,在中饋,貞吉 [25, 家人: 六二]). This verse highlights the late Bronze Age belief that a family's good fortune and well-being are intimately tied to a wife's diligence in home cooking. Likely due in part to this statement in the *Yi Jing*, subsequent usages of the term "*zhongkui*" in Chinese history come imbued with ideas about women's responsibilities and duties in domestic cuisine. There is no doubt that this was the intended effect of its use in the title.

Most modern academic publications date Madame Wu's work to the late Southern Song dynasty, though some believe it was written during the beginning of the Mongol Yuan dynasty, thus placing the date of the work several decades around 1279, the official beginning of the Yuan dynasty. Although not specified in the edition of *Shuofu* anthology used for this translation, some transcripts of unspecified *Wushi Zhongkuilu* editions include the character "宋" (*Song*) as part of its title, which would specify both Northen and Southern Song dynasty (960–1279 CE). Needless to say, dating this work is challenging, not least since the *Shuofu* anthology was published near the end of the Yuan dynasty[1] and how its author Tao Zongyi 陶宗儀 came across Madame Wu's manuscript is altogether unknown. Moreover, although her work was included among numerous other Song period works, the anthology also contains much earlier works from the Tang dynasty and Five dynasties period (五代十國). Indeed, the spread of possible dates for when Madame Wu's work was written is potentially quite large. Still, we must concede that others with expertise in this matter have likely spent more time pinpoint-

---

[1] Those interested in the history of this vast anthology may like Christopher P. Atwoods work on the subject "The Textual History of Tao Zongyi's Shuofu"[2]

ing this date, and thus we will refer to the Southern Song dynasty as the period of the work's creation.

Taken all together, a recomposed translation of the title of the *Wushi Shoungkuilu* cookbook would be: "The records on essential matters of domestic cuisine by a madame born of surname Wu from *Pujiang* in Eastern China, and is believed to have live around the end of Southern Song dynasty". It's a mouthful but nevertheless descriptive.

A Note on Culinary Works by Chinese Women

The role of Chinese women in the culinary traditions of China cannot be understated. In most households throughout Chinese history, women traditionally ran the kitchens, but the number of written culinary works by them is minuscule compared to all that men wrote. Indeed, throughout China's thousands of years of culinary development until the end of its dynastic era (in the early 1910s), there have only been **four** known Chinese culinary works of women's authorship. We provide a very brief outline of the works here in hopes that this could spur further study on the subject.

Perhaps the earliest known cookbook that has a Chinese woman as a direct collaborator or author is the Chishi Shijing 崔氏食經. The work was believed to have been compiled by the scholar and a high official of the Northern Wei dynasty (386-535 CE) Cui Hao 崔浩, and partially written by his mother. In what remains of the work's preface, Cui indicated that he and his mother wanted to preserve the family's recipes amid the period's turmoils. Sadly, Cui and his household did not survive the era's politics and were put to death by the Wei Emperor. The original culinary work was either destroyed or lost. Chinese food historiographers, such as Osamu Shinoda, nevertheless believed that the ancient editors eventually repurposed parts of this work into the fermentation and food processing chapters of the *Qimin Yaoshu* 齊民要術 (544 CE) and thus it still exists, albeit in a fragmented and reconstituted form [13, p.125]. If accurate, the sheer impact of the knowledge imparted by Cui's mother on the development of Chinese cuisine cannot be overstated, especially considering that the *Qimin Yaoshu* is the predominant and arguably most influential of all historical Chinese agricultural texts.

After this, there would be several more centuries until near the end of the Song dynasty, for publication of the *Wushi Zhongkuilu* 吳氏中饋錄, of with which this present English publication is concerned. Again, the text provides a crucial window revealing the essential aspects of medieval Chinese cuisines, such as how integral food preservation was to the home cooking of the time and the cosmopolitan nature of the foods consumed.

Following this, we would have to wait another 700 years to the 1800s Qing dynasty before seeing two more culinary books published by Chinese women. Both books were also named "*Zhongkuilu*", likely a description of their subject matter while invoking the earlier Song dynasty work. The author of the first of the two works is a remarkable women scholar, Peng Songyu 彭崧毓, who competed and ranked near the top in the imperial examinations. The author of the second, more well-studied work was Zeng Yi 曾懿, and both the life of the author and her work were discussed in detail in Jin Feng's article "*The Female Chef and the Nation*" [10],

Those interested in the subject could use Jin Feng's work as a starting point, as well as the works of Xi Lifeng 奚丽芳, whose fascinating 2017 manuscript goes into detail on the aims of women's cookbook [21]. Xi's recent work examining the comparative differences between men's and women's cookbook writing is also quite insightful [22].

Considering the critical roles of women in developing Chinese cuisine and the relatively limited work done studying the cookbooks and historical culinary works by Chinese women, much more could be learned if only we redirected more academic and research attention to this area. We eagerly look forward to more developments and publications on the subject matter in the future.

CONTENTS

Foreword
  By Eugene N. Anderson   i

Foreword
  By Miranda Brown   vii

Translator's Preface
  By Sean J.S. Chen   ix

A Note on Units of Measurement   xv

A Note on the Original Title   xix

A Note on Culinary Works by Chinese Women   xxiii

Preserved Meats and Pickled Fish   1
  Raw Crab 3
  Seared fish 4
  Water-pickled fish 5
  Pickled meat 6
  Smashed cucumber 7
  Counting rods cured meat 8
  Stove-baked chicken 9

Steamed shad 10
Curing pork during the summer months 11
Wind-cured fish 12
"Raw" pork 13
Fish sauce 14
Jiu-lees pig's head, knuckles, and trotters 15
Jiu marinated shrimp 16
Pressed razor clams 17
Drunken crab 18
Sun-dried shrimp that stays red 19
Cooking fish 20
Keeping the colour of cooked crab green and cleaning
    clams 21
Making meat sauce 22
Pickled yellow sparrows 23
Techniques for processing food 24

Preparing Vegetables   29

Salted gourd and beans 31
Eggplant steamed with sugar 33
Stuffed cucumber 34
Garlic cucumber 35
Thrice-cooked cucumber 36
Dried garlic shoots 37
Stored mustard greens 38
Piquant mustard juice 39
Soy-paste Buddha's hand citron, citron, and pear 40
Eggplant in *jiu*-lees 41
Radish in *jiu*-lees 42
Ginger in *jiu*-lees 43
Preparing garlic shoots 44
Three-harmonies vegetables 45
Quick chopped bits 46
Carrots preserved in red ferment starter 47
Garlic greens 48

Making plain dried eggplant 49
Soy-paste pickled cucumber 50
Dried greens in sealed-jars 51
Tossed mixed greens 52
Steamed dried vegetable 53
Quail eggplants 54
Shixiang eggplants 55
Jiu-lees eggplant 57
Jiaobai preserved in red ferment starter 58
Sweet and sour eggplant 59
Garlic winter melon 60
Curing salted garlic chives 61
Making *gu* greens 62
Napa cabbage 63
Inverted greens 64
Dried bamboo shoots 66
Mild sun-dried bamboo shoots 67
Making *jiu douchi* 68
Water *douchi* 69
Red salt beans 70
Garlic ume 72

Sweet Foods   73

Making toasted wheat flour 75
Flour halva 76
Snowflake pastries 77
Making *Saboni* 78
Short pastries 80
Fried sandwiched pastries 81
Little pressed short pastries 82
Five fragrance cakes 83
Boiled sandy balls 84
Zongzi 85
Jade-filled lung 86
Wontons 87

Slippery water noodles 88
Thin sugar crisps 89
Sugar torreya 90

Glossary   91

Bibliography   99

Index   103

Chapter I

Preserved Meats and Pickled Fish
脯鮓

Madame Wu's Handbook on Home-Cooking

RAW CRAB

Chop up raw crab, simmer first in sesame oil until done, and let cool. Take black cardamom, fennel, *sharen*, Sichuan pepper powder, young ginger[1], and pepper[2] and grind them into a powder. Then add green onion, salt, and vinegar. Take these ten flavours together and mix in with the crab,[3] then serve immediately.

蟹生[4]

用生蟹剁碎,以麻油先熬熟,冷,并草果、茴香、砂仁、花椒末、水薑、胡椒俱為末,再加葱、鹽、醋共十味,入蟹內拌勻,即時可食。

---

[1] Translated here as "young ginger", the Chinese term in the text is literally "water ginger". The term likely denotes the very young and fresh ginger similar to that used for making *gari* ガリ, or "Japanese pickled ginger", which is sweet and light in taste due to its higher sugar and water content.

[2] In early modern China, white pepper (*Piper nigrum*) was more commonly used, though this may or may not be the case in further back in Song dynasty.

[3] The Chinese text here indicates that the seasoning mixture should be put "...into the crab and mixed evenly". While this may describe adding and mixing seasonings into the crab's carapace for eating, the fact that the crab was chopped up likely means the seasonings were just mixed into a bowl with all the chunks of chopped crab.

[4] This is a raw crab salad, with similarities to the raw fish dishes known as *kuai* 膾 (or alternatively, 鱠) that were immensely popular during much of the Chinese dynastic periods. These were likely related to Japanese *sashimi* 刺身 and Korean *hoe* 회. Consumption of raw fish *kuai* in Chinese culture tapered during late Ming and Early Qing dynasty likely due to known health issues caused by parasites from prepared raw fish. Still, there are many Chinese cultures that continue to consume *kuai*, namely those of the Guangzhou, Fujian, Nanhai, and Northern Vietnamese geographies. Overseas communities with ancestry from these regions also consume Chinese raw fish dishes, but they are now typically referred to as *yusheng* (魚生, lit. *fish raw*) or *shengyupian* (生魚片, lit. *raw fish slices*) rather than *kuai*.

吳氏中饋錄

SEARED FISH

Clean newly caught Grenadier Anchovies, and broil them over charcoal until completely dried, then store them. Another way to prepare them is to remove their heads and tails, cut them into segments, and fry them in oil until done. Wrap the pieces in bamboo leaves[5], place them into an earthenware pot until full, and seal the pot with clay.

炙魚[6]

鱭魚新出水者治淨,炭上十分炙乾,收藏。一法:以鱭魚去頭尾,切作段,用油炙熟。每服[7],用箬間盛瓦礶內,泥封。

---

[5] Specifically, the leaves of *Indocalamus tessellatus*, a species of broadleaf bamboo. This is the plant whose leaves are used for wrapping Chinese *zongzi* (a filled "dumpling" similar in concept to the Mexican tamale) and gives the food a unique aroma reminiscent of dried hay and wood.

[6] The character *zhi* 炙 is somewhat tricky to interpret since the culinary technique it refers to differs depending on context. In this recipe, it was used to describe both broiling the fish over charcoal or frying it in oil over high heat. Although translated here as "seared", it could describe a wide variety of dry (non-aqueous) cooking techniques, where the food is cooked at a very high heat until browned.

[7] The character "服" indicates an arbitrary unit and could be read as "a bunch". Alternatively, it could be a very old mis-transcription and should be read as "each piece" (段), in which case, the pieces were individually wrapped.

WATER-PICKLED FISH

For curing, cut a medium carp[8] into large pieces and wipe them dry. For each *jin* of carp, rub with four *liang* of toasted salt and let them marinate overnight. Rinse them clean and let them dry in the breeze. Next, mix them well with two *liang* of salt and one *jin* of *jiu*-lees and place them inside an earthenware urn. Seal it with paper, bamboo leaves, and an application of clay.

水醃魚[9]

臘中鯉魚切大塊,拭乾。一斤用炒鹽四兩擦過,淹一宿,洗淨晾乾,再用鹽二兩、糟一斤,拌勻,入瓮,紙、箬、泥封塗。

---

[8]There is some question on interpreting the first part of this sentence, which literally translates as "Curing medium carp, cut into big pieces." This part could be read as "To cure a medium carp, cut it into big pieces" or "Cut a carp in the middle of its curing into big pieces." The former seems more likely, though it is impossible to verify this directly.

[9]I used the literal translation for the title, but the "water" is more likely referring to this recipe's rather liquidy end product. Because many *jiu*-lees contain high concentrations of proteolytic enzymes, their addition would have transformed the flesh of the carp into something quite soft and soaking in its own liquid.

吳氏中饋錄

Pickled meat

Boil the raw pork or mutton leg and carefully shave off slices. Use the back[10] of the knife to evenly pound them two or three times and cut them into irregularly shaped pieces. When the soup boils, they must be removed and left to drain, then wrung dry inside a cloth. For each *jin* add one *zhan* of vinegar, four *qian* of salt, and a little of Sichuan pepper oil, black cardamom, and *sharen*. This is a delightful dish for eating together.

肉鮓[11]

生燒[12]豬羊腿,精批作片,以刀背勻搥三兩次、切作塊子。沸湯隨漉出,用布內扭乾。每一斤入好醋一盞,鹽四錢,椒油、草果、砂仁各少許,供饌亦珍美。

---

[10] Pounding the slices of cooked meat with the back/spine of the knife two or three times will likely tenderize the tougher cuts of pork or mutton used here. The industrially farmed meats of modern times may very well shred if given two or three strokes with the back of the knife. The latter meats would likely do better if lightly tenderized or flattened with the broadsides of the Chinese kitchen knife.

[11] The character *zha* (鮓) is typically used to describe a preserving or seasoning method for fish, employing salt and *jiu*-lees similar to Japanese *kasuzuke* 粕漬け. In this case, pork or mutton was used instead and pickled with vinegar, salt, and spices. The same character was also used to describe foods pickled with red rice ferment starter (紅麴米, hongqumi) and salt (See *Carrots preserved in red ferment starter* on page 47) though this was not always the case (See *Dried bamboo shoots* on page 66). As hinted by the radical of the character, it was typically done with fish though the method can also be applied to other vegetables and meats.

[12] The *shao* (燒) translates literally to "burn". However, when used to describe cooking techniques, it could mean everything from plain "cooking", to broiling, as well as boiling, much like the English word "brew" could mean everything from to decoct, infuse, or ferment. The logic of using the term is that the item being cooked is being held to a burning flame directly or via a container. As such, one can say you are going to "burn boiled water" (燒開水, shaokaishui) or "burn vegetables/dishes" (燒菜, shaocai) to describe boiling water and cooking vegetables, respectively. By looking at the whole recipe, we see that the author likely intended the meat to be boiled, not roasted or broiled.

SMASHED CUCUMBER

Take the same quantities of soy-paste pickled cucumber[13], raw ginger, the white portions of green onions, light-flavoured dried bamboo shoots or *jiaobai*, dried shrimp, and chicken breast. Slice them into long thin strips, stir-fry them in "fragrant oil"[14], and serve.

瓜齏

醬瓜[15]、生薑、蔥白、淡筍乾或茭白、鰕米、雞胸肉各等分，切作長條絲兒，香油炒過，供之。

---

[13] This pickled cucumber likely has some similarities to Japanese *misozuke* 味噌漬け, which is simply cucumber covered in miso (another fermented soy-paste) and left to cure.

[14] In modern Chinese usage, *xiangyou* (香油) almost always refers to sesame oil. However, it is unclear whether the same was true during Song dynasty.

[15] Though 瓜 could refer to any gourd, the one that was most likely used was the ubiquitous cucumber. As a vegetable, cucumber was already well established in China by the Song dynasty after being introduced via the Silk Road ten centuries prior from India during the Han dynasty. The Ming dynasty *Bencao Gangmu* 本草綱目 has a section dedicated to gourds and should be read by anyone interested in the subject [28, vol. 28, part 3].

吳氏中饋錄

COUNTING RODS CURED MEAT

Cut a piece of pork containing lean and fatty parts into pieces three *cun* long strips, in the manner of counting rods. Blend together granulated sugar, ground Sichuan pepper, and ground susha. Mix it evenly with the pork, sun-dry them, and steam them until done.[16]

算條巴子[17]

豬肉精肥，冬[18]另切作三寸長，各如算子[19]樣，以砂糖、花椒末、宿砂末調和得所，拌勻、晒乾、蒸熟。

---

[16] It is heartening to see the Chinese method of steaming dry-cured meats has such a long history. Indeed, even now, steaming dried hams and sausages is the preferred preparation method when directly consuming the cured item.

[17] The term *bazi* 巴子 describes a dry-cured item, typically made of meat. The use of the word *ba* for such items has such a lengthy history that there are distinct compound characters for *ba* noting the animal from which it is made, specifically "羓", "鲌", and "豝" for sheep, fish and pork, respectively. Seeing that the term *ba* is used to describe dried items, the words for rice cracking (*ba*, 粑) or a scab on a wound (*ba*, 疤) are likely etymologically related.

[18] This character is likely an ancient transcription or typesetting error and should be "各" (*ge*, lit. each/every), since "winter" (*dong*, 冬) would not make would sense here.

[19] Before the popularization of the bead abacus during the Ming dynasty, almost all arithmetic calculations in China were done using sets of thin counting sticks (算條/算子, suantiao/suanzi), typically around 0.5cm in diameter and 15cm in length. These sticks were arranged on a board in different configurations to represent any integers, with digits 0 to 9 placed in decimal positions as we do for Arabic numerals. Numerical computations were performed through a manual algorithm for arranging these rods into their different digit configurations, and the results from the computation process were recorded in the formal Chinese numeral system to convey the numbers in written documents. The rod computation system is now a relic of the past, though its continuing influence is seen in the Suzhou numerals, which is a written the numeral system is still used for denoting prices in traditional Chinese markets and restaurants.

Stove-baked Chicken

Take one chicken and boil it in water until 80% done, and chop it into small pieces. Add a little oil into a wok and heat it, place the chicken inside to stir-fry briefly, then use a large metal vessel or wooden bowl to cover it. Heat it up well, then add the same quantity of both vinegar and *jiu* along with some salt and continue cooking. Wait until the liquids have reduced and cook further. When this is done several times, the dish will be very tender and thoroughly done and ready to eat.

爐焙雞

用鷄一隻，水煮八分熟，剁作小塊。鍋內放油少許，燒热，放鷄在內略炒，以錠[20]子或椀[21]盍定。燒及熱，醋、酒相半，入鹽少許，烹[22]之。候乾，再烹。如此數次，候十分酥熟取用。

---

[20] The character *ding* 錠 refers to a metal board or plate that would not be too helpful for covering the chicken. But considering the character indicates something of metallic composition, and that to cover the food, this object should be effectively in the form of a spacious dome, perhaps this references a metal pot or wok-like vessel similar to the homophonic Chinese *ding* 鼎.

[21] The character here specifies a wooden bowl (note its wood radical 木) and not your typical stoneware bowls (*wan*, 碗) with the stone radical (石).

[22] Translated here as simply "cook", *peng* 烹 describes a technique where a mostly cooked item is further quickly cooked with liquid seasonings and stirred. This could be considered a stir-frying but with more liquids involved.

吳氏中饋錄

STEAMED SHAD

Shad is a fish which one cleans by removing the innards but not its scales.[23] Use a cloth to wipe away any bloody liquids and place it in a large flat bowl.[24] Crush Sichuan pepper, *sharen*, and soy-paste in a mortar, mixed with water, *jiu*, and green onion and season it. Steam it, remove its scales, and eat with everyone.

蒸鰣魚

鰣魚去腸不去鱗,用布拭去血水,放盪鑼內,以花椒、砂仁、醬擂碎,水、酒、葱拌勻,其味和,蒸之。去鱗,供食。

---

[23] The practice of steaming shad with its scales on is considered a canonical way of preparing this fish, even today. The rationale is that the removal of the scales before cooking disrupts the tissues of the fish sufficiently that its flavours and textures would be ruined since the oils and proteins under its skin would be lost during the cooking process. Some have also rationalized that the scales of this fish are thin enough to consume whole or that spitting the scales out during the meal could be considered part of the joy of eating shad. Dr. Anderson has indicated that it is also customary not to scale shad in some parts of the United States before consumption.

[24] The Chinese name of this bowl is a *tangluo* 湯鑼, which translates as a "soup gong". This container could be thought of as either a plate with raised edges or a large flat bowl.

Curing pork during the summer months

Rub a piece of pork using hot salt that has been toasted and ensure it is evenly applied. Place it in a jar, press it with a rock overnight, and then hang it up. If there are traces of liquids on it, then use a large rock to further press it dry and hang it in a windy location. When thus prepared, the meat will not spoil.

夏月醃肉法

用炒過熱鹽擦肉，令軟勻。[25]下缸內，石壓一夜，掛起。見水痕即以大石壓乾，挂當風處。不敗。

---

[25] *Ruanyun* 軟勻, literally "soft evenly", probably alludes to a technique where one gently massages the salt onto the chunk of meat.

吳氏中饋錄

Wind-cured fish

Take either a black carp[26] or common carp[27] and remove its innards. For each *jin* of fish, marinade with four or five *qian* of salt for seven days. Remove, rinse it clean, and wipe it dry. Slice the fish under its gills and rub the insides of the gill and the abdominal cavity with a mixture of Sichuan pepper, fennel, and toasted salt. Wrap the outside with paper and run a strand of hemp fibre[28] though several fish to thread them into a bunch. Hang in a windy location. The more of the mixture one stuffs into the abdomen of the fish, the better the results.

風魚法

用青魚、鯉魚破去腸胃,每斤用鹽四五錢,醃七日。取起,洗淨,拭乾[29]。腮下切一刀,將川椒、茴香加炒鹽,擦入腮內并腹裏,外以紙包裹,外用麻皮扎成一箇[30]。挂于當風之處,腹內入料多些方妙

---

[26] *Mylopharyngodon piceus*

[27] *Cyprinus carpio*

[28] *Mapi* 麻皮 are the long ribbons of fibres pulled from harvested hemp, which are further processed into other products like rope or string. These fibres are derived from the bast of the hemp plant, which are longitudinal fibres running the length of the hemp plant between the the core of its stem and the cortex/skin of the plant.

[29] The character "乾" in the term "拭乾" should be read with its alternative pronunciation *gan*, which means "to be dry", rather than its typical pronunciation *qian* (meaning "sun-light/masculine"), which would be nonsensical here. This alternative pronunciation should be used when reading this Ming dynasty edition of the cookbook.

[30] The choice of writing this character of *ge* as "箇" rather than its more common form "個" is quite notable. Namely, by using the character form containing the bamboo radical "⺮", the former character directly alludes to the plant matter binding the fish into a unit mass rather than the latter character which uses a less relevant character with a person radical "亻".

"Raw" pork

Take lean pork, cut it into thin slices, and rinse them clean with soy-sauce. Heat a wok to red hot and rapidly stir-fry the pork to rid it of its bloody liquids. When its colour turns off-white, it is done. Remove them from the wok and slice them into thin slivers. Next combine it with soy-paste pickled cucumber, vinegar pickled radish, garlic, *sharen*, black cardamom, Sichuan pepper, slivers of mandarin peel, and "fragrant oil", then mix while stir-frying. When the pork slivers are about to be served, add vinegar to it and mix evenly. This dish is a delight to eat.[31]

肉生法

用精肉切細薄片子,醬油洗淨[32],入火燒紅鍋、爆炒,去血水、微白,即好。取出,切成絲,再加醬瓜、糟蘿蔔、大蒜、砂仁、草果、花椒、橘絲、香油拌炒。肉絲臨食加醋和勻,食之甚美。

---

[31] Despite the dish's name, one quickly notices that there is no raw pork in it. Taking this into consideration, this may be a name derived from an older dish that historically used raw pork but was modified to this version for health reasons.

[32] This ambiguous statement could either refer to rinsing the meat clean with soy-sauce or rinsing it clean of soy-sauce that was previously applied. We have chosen to go with the former. Nevertheless, considering the relative rarity of soy-sauce production in Song dynasty, either of them seems rather extravagant.

吳氏中饋錄

Fish sauce

Use a fish weighing one *jin*. After chopping the fish into a mince and rinsing it, mix it evenly with three *liang* of toasted salt, one *qian* of Sichuan pepper, one *qian* of fennel, one *qian* of dried ginger, two *qian* of divine starter,[33] five *qian* of red ferment starter, and *jiu*. Fill it into a porcelain flask and seal well. It can be used after ten days.[34] Add a small amount of chopped green onions to it when eating.[35]

魚醬法

用魚一斤，切碎洗淨後，炒鹽三兩、花椒一錢、茴香一錢、乾姜一錢、神麴二錢、紅麴五錢，加酒和勻拌魚肉，入磁瓶封好，十日可用。吃時加蔥花少許。

---

[33] Divine starter was a specific type of Chines *qu* (麴) starter culture consisting of a mixture of fungi and yeast varieties and primarily used to ferment grain to produce *jiu*. Each type of starter, with its distinctive mixture of microorganisms, gave the resulting product a unique flavour profile, and some may have been passed down through families as part of their heirloom. The Divine starter appeared to be quite popular in the past, enough that several versions were described in the seventh scroll of the 6th-century agricultural manual, the *Qimin Yaoshu* 齊民要術.

[34] The addition of salt preserves the fish and controls the type of bacteria fermenting the fish, while the addition of the starters introduces fungi and yeasts that break down the flesh of the fish and bring flavour to the sauce through their released enzymes and fermentation by-products. This combination of salt, fermentation starters, and protein is remarkably similar to soy-sauce production. If one removed everything in this brewing recipe except the salt, the wheat containing divine starter, and added some water, one could probably produce a white "soy" sauce similar to that of Japanese *shiro shoyu* 白醬油.

[35] This recipe may very well have been a distant ancestor of our modern tomato ketchup, which resulted after a series of creations initially "inspired" by the fish sauces imported from Southeast Asia. Texture-wise, this sauce is likely thicker and more similar to a fermented fish paste to the likes of Cambodian *prahok*.

Jiu-LEES PIG'S HEAD, KNUCKLES, AND TROTTERS

Use pig's heads, knuckles or trotters, boil them until completely soft, and remove their bones. Spread out a cloth to wrap the meat, weight the meat down flat with a large rock, and let it press for a night. It is very good when *jiu*-lees are used. [36]

糟豬頭、蹄、爪法

用豬頭、蹄、爪,煮爛,去骨。布包攤開,大石壓扁,實落一宿,糟用甚佳。

---

[36] This dish is basically a marinated head cheese. If it is anything similar to modern preparations, the person making it would probably pack *jiu*-lees around the meat as it is being weighed down to marinade it.

吳氏中饋錄

Jiu MARINATED SHRIMP

Use large shrimp that have not been rinsed and cut off their antennae and tails. For each *jin*, use five *qian* of salt and marinate for half a day. Strain dry and put them into a flask. Repeat, putting down one layer of shrimp, then thirty grains of Sichuan pepper, the more peppercorns the better. One could also mix the Sichuan pepper with the shrimp and put them into the flask with similarly good results. When the shrimp is in the flask, dissolve three *liang* of salt into good *jiu* for every *jin* of shrimp, pour the liquid into the flask, and seal the flask's opening with a clay cap. In spring and autumn, this dish will be good to eat in five to seven days. In the winter, it will be ready in ten days.[37]

酒醃蝦法

用大蝦不見水洗,剪去鬚尾。每斤用鹽五錢,淹半日,瀝乾,入瓶中。蝦一層,放椒三十粒,以椒多為妙。或用椒拌蝦,裝入瓶中亦妙。裝完,每斤用鹽三兩,好酒化開,澆入瓶內,封好泥頭。春秋五七日,即好吃。冬月十日方好。

---

[37] The fact that the author did not mention summer here could mean that this dish is not suitable for preparation during warmer times of the year

Pressed razor clams

Take one *jin* of razor clams, mix with two *liang* of salt, and marinade for a day. Wash them clean, flick them dry, wrap them in cloth, and press them with a large stone. To them, add five *qian* of cooked oil,[38] five *qian* each of ginger and sliced strips of mandarin peel, one *qian* of salt, five *fen* of green onion slivers, and one generous *zhan* of *jiu*, one *ge* of rice congee[39], and ground rice[40]. Mix evenly and fill them into a flask. Seal the flask with clay for ten days and it is ready to serve. The method for preparing pressed fish is the same.

蟶鮓

蟶一斤，鹽一兩，醃一伏時。再洗淨，控乾，布包石壓，加熟油五錢，薑、橘絲五錢、鹽一錢、蔥絲五分，酒一大盞，飯糝一合，磨米拌勻入瓶，泥封十日可供。魚鮓同。

---

[38] It is unclear whether the "cooked oil" was hot when all the other ingredients were added. However, considering that this is an uncooked pickled dish similar to pressed fish, it most likely points to using a hot pressed oil (as with many Chinese seed oils) or simply plain oil that has been heated and left to cool.

[39] Translated here as "rice congee", *fan san* 飯糝 could mean either plain cooked rice or rice that has been prepared using broth or soup.

[40] Since the author specified no quantity for the ground rice and the amount used was up to the cook, I suspect its primary purpose was not for flavour or texture but to absorb excess moisture. Perhaps this ground rice was the toasted type, similar to the ones used for famous fenzheng pork (*fenshung rou*, 粉蒸肉) or Thai larb ลาบ.

吳氏中饋錄

Drunken crab

By adding "fragrant oil"[41] to soy-sauce, it allows one to keep it around without it becoming grainy.[42] Add a bowl each of *jiu*-lees, vinegar, *jiu*, and soy-sauce. If there are many crabs, add in another small dish of salt. Another excellent recipe for making drunken crabs is to use seven bowls of *jiu*, three bowls of vinegar, and two bowls of salt.

醉蟹

香油入醬油內，亦可久留，不砂。[43]糟、醋、酒、醬各一碗，蟹多，加鹽一碟。又法：用酒七碗、醋三碗、鹽二碗，醉蟹亦妙。

---

[41] Considering that the previous crab dish used sesame oil, the ambiguous term "fragrant oil" here likely also refers to sesame oil.

[42] What is likely being suggested here is that adding oil prevents the water in the soy-sauce from evaporating, and this inhibits crystallization of the salts in the soy-sauce.

[43] It is odd that a recipe for drunken crab starts with advice on how to preserve soy-sauce. It certainly makes one wonder if medieval transcriptions or copy-and-paste issues occurred in this part of the text.

Sun-dried shrimp that stays red

Stir-fry shrimp with salt until done, place them in a straining basket and douse with well water to wash away the salt, then dry them. Its colour will stay red and not change.[44]

晒蝦不變紅色[45]

蝦用鹽炒熟，盛籩內，用井水淋，洗去鹽，晒乾。色紅不變。

---

[44] Strictly speaking, this is more a tip for processing shrimp and less of an actual recipe for a dish.

[45] The title translates to "Sun-dried shrimp that does not turn red", but looking at the recipe tells us that this is not the actual meaning of that title. Instead, "unchanging red" (不變紅色) refers to a red colour that does not change or fade away. Indeed, boiling shrimp in concentrated brine before drying is standard practice for making dried shrimp (*xiami* 蝦米) that stays a bright reddish-orange and does not fade with storage. Perhaps this shows an earlier variation of our modern technique for making dried shrimp.

吳氏中饋錄

Cooking fish

When cooking river fish in the typical manner, boiling them first in water will render their bones tender. For fish from large rivers and the sea, seasoning their boiling stock first before being putting them in the pot will keep their bones firm.

煮魚法

凡煮河魚，先下水下燒，則骨酥。江海魚先調滾汁下鍋，則骨堅也。

Keeping the Colour of Cooked Crab Green and Cleaning Clams

Take three to five persimmon calyces[46] and cook them with the crab to retain its blue-green colour. After that, cook the clams with the kernels of loquat seeds to thoroughly clean them.[47]

煮蟹青色、蛤俐脫丁

用柿蒂三、五個同蟹煮,色青,後用枇杷核內仁同蛤蜊煮,脫丁。

---

[46]The persimmon fruit calyx is the green leaf-like portion on top of the fruit, previously the flower's sepals. They are used in traditional Chinese medicine to cure stomach ailments, including as an antiemetic to prevent vomiting. The calyx contains a fair amount of tannins, which, on top of their pharmacologic effect when taken, may help preserve the crab's colour.

[47]Translated literally as "removing the nails/small bits", the term *tuoding* 脫丁 likely denotes the important step in cleaning the acquired clams of mud, debris, and its byssus such that it can be enjoyably consumed. The only place that appears to use this obscure term at present is at some Chaozhou fisheries, where they use it to describe the cleaning and processing of a thin-shelled shellfish *Musculus senhousei*.

吳氏中饋錄

MAKING MEAT SAUCE

Remove the tendons and bones from four *jin* of lean meat. Take one *jin* and eight *liang* of soy-paste, four *liang* of finely ground salt, a bowl of the white portions of green onions, finely chopped, and five or six *qian* each of Sichuan pepper, fennel, and dried mandarin peel, then grind and mix them with *jiu* and the meat, such that the mixture has the texture of thick congee. Place it into an urn and seal it well. Let it rest under the hot sun for more than ten days, then open the seal to take a look. If it is too dry, add more *jiu*. If it tastes bland, add more salt. Seal again with clay and let it rest under the sun.[48]

造肉醬

精肉四斤去筋骨,醬一斤八兩,研細鹽四兩,蔥白細切一碗,川椒、茴香、陳皮各五六 [錢],用酒拌各粉并肉如稠粥,入罈,封固。晒烈日中,十餘日,開看,乾,再加酒。淡,再加鹽。又,封以泥晒之。

---

[48] Think of this as a spicier fish sauce made with meat. Note the addition of soy paste, which adds a large amount of proteolytic enzymes to the mixture and likely steers this sauce's flavour profile closer to a soy-sauce.

Pickled yellow sparrows

Clean each one well, wash them with *jiu*, wipe them dry, and do not let them come in contact with water. Combine "yellowed wheat"[49], red ferment starter, salt, Sichuan pepper, and slivered green onion together until the desired flavour is obtained. Next place the sparrows into a flat urn, alternating with a layer of the meat and a layer of the seasoning, then pack it down well. Cover the jar with bamboo shoots sheaths and secure it with skewers of bamboo slats. When the pickling juice starts to pool, pour it all out, and add *jiu* to completely soak them. Seal tightly for long-term use.

黃雀[50]鮓

每隻治淨,用酒洗,拭乾,不犯水。用麥黃、紅麴、鹽、椒、葱絲,嘗味和為止。却將雀入匾罈內;鋪一層,上料一層,裝實。以箬蓋篾片芊定。候滷出,傾去,加酒浸,密封久用。

---

[49] The Ming dynasty *Bencao Gangmu* indicated that *maihuang* 麥黃 is a combination of rice and wheat flour steamed until they are caramelized to a yellow colour. It is unclear if this term had the same meaning in Song dynasty. Steam caramelization is still regularly done to transform white *mianxian* 麵線, a type of pulled wheat pasta, into red *mianxian* in Fujian and Taiwan, the latter being able to endure prolonged cooking in soups without turning to mush or melting away. Alternatively, this could also be wheat grains cultured with koji mould and attained a coat of yellow spores similar to *huangzi* 黃子, or soybeans cultured with koji mould.

[50] Strictly speaking, *huangque* are not yellow sparrows but colloquially refer to any number of small yellow passerine songbirds in Chinese-language speaking localities. Depending on geographic region, these could range from the Eurasian siskin (*Spinus spinus*) to the Yellow breasted bunting (*Emberiza aureola*), though in formal Chinese biological terminology, *huangque* refers to the former. For simplicity, we translate them here as simply: "sparrows".

吳氏中饋錄

TECHNIQUES FOR PROCESSING FOOD

- Clean pork stomachs with flour and clean pork intestines with granulated sugar. Done in this manner, they will not smell.[51]

- When cooking the bamboo shoots, add mint and a small quantity of salt or wood ash[52] so that they will not taste unpleasant.

- When pickling crab, add half a piece of vegetal soap on top of the urn,[53] and it will keep for a long time.

- When cleaning fish, add a drop or two of oil and it will not become sticky with mucus. When cooking fish, add some powdered myrrh, and it will not turn rank.[54]

---

[51] *Qi* 氣 here is likely referring to the rank smells of the pork innards. Cleaning pork stomachs with flour is still common centuries later, but cleaning pork intestines with sugar is now rare.

[52] Processing bamboo shoots with wood ash or its filtrate is crucial for making the shoots of certain bamboo species edible. This technique is common enough and is recorded in various texts including the Northern Song Bamboo-shoot manual (*Sunpu*, 筍譜) of Shi Zanning 釋贊寧.

[53] The vegetal soap here is most likely extracted from the Chinese honey locust tree *Gleditsia sinensis*, also known as the soap bean tree. The soap is a saponin-rich extract from the pulp of the tree's seed pods and can be used for washing clothes or hair. Whether the "half a piece/spindle" (*banding*, 半錠) here refers to simply an opened-up pod or a piece of a refined soap-like product is unclear.

[54] The antiseptic properties of myrrh would certainly help inhibit bacterial growth. Though not particularly delightful, the resin's bitter aroma also likely helps cover the smell of fish that has started to go off.

Madame Wu's Handbook on Home-Cooking

- When cooking goose, add many cherry leaves and the goose will become tender easily.

- When cooking well aged cured pork, once it is done, take numerous chucks of red-hot charcoal and add them into the pot. Done in this manner it will not have the smell of rancid oil.

- When cooking various sorts of meat, seal the pot well and add one or two mulberry fruits, the meat will become tender easily and quite fragrant.

- During the summer months, meats cooked solely in vinegar last for ten days.

- With noodles, it is not advisable to put it through cold unboiled water. Rather, use boiled water that has been left until cold to cool them for eating.[55]

---

[55] This states that the cook should submerge freshly cooked hot noodles in cooled boiled water for eating, but not in cold, unboiled water. Cooling cooked noodles is still commonly done in many East Asian cuisines. Short of reducing the noodle's temperature, it also firms up its texture after cooking and improves overall mouthfeel. While most people nowadays cool the noodles in tap water, considering the pathogens and variable water quality that existed before modern sanitation, this is certainly sound advice.

吳氏中饋錄

- When grilling meat[56] avoid using mulberry wood for fuel[57].

- For crab pickled in soy-paste or *jiu*-lees, do not expose it to lantern light, otherwise it will become grainy in texture.

- If the *jiu* has soured, take one *sheng* of azuki beans, toast them thoroughly to a dark-brown, bag them, and put them into the vat, and all will be well.

- The dilute alkaline solution collected from dye mills[58] can be sun dried and used to envelope fresh cucumber and eggplants such that they can be eaten during winter months.

- Wrap mandarins in pine needles and they will not dry for three or four months. One can also do this by storing mandarins in mung beans.

---

[56] This is most likely not "grilled" in the technical sense of the word, but rather, skewered and cooked over the high heat of either bare flames or charcoal. Though not technically accurate, it is translated thus for ease of reading.

[57] Why one should not use mulberry wood is unclear, though it could be due to the speed and temperature in which it burns or the flavours it imparts onto the grilled items.

[58] The dyeing mills described were probably using indigo, and the "dripped diluted ash" (瀝過淡灰) was most likely the supernatant left from producing indigo dye. The *Qimin Yaoshu* described the process in detail, where the fermented liquids from the indigo plant were reacted with calcium hydroxide or calcium oxide and left so the particles of indigo dye could settle out of the liquid [31, vol. 5] (種藍第五十三: 著石灰一斗五升，急手抨之，一食頃止。澄清，瀉去水，別作小坑，貯藍澱著坑中).

治食有法

- 洗豬肚用麵，洗豬臟用砂糖，不氣。
- 煮笋入薄荷，少加鹽或以灰，則不蔹[59]。
- 糟蟹，罈上加皂角半錠，可留久。
- 洗魚滴生油一二點，則無涎。煮魚下末香，不腥。
- 煮鶩，下櫻桃葉數片，易軟。
- 煮陳臘肉，將熟，取燒紅炭，投數塊入鍋內，則不油蔹[60]氣。
- 煮諸般肉封鍋口，用楮實子一二粒同煮，易爛又香。
- 夏月肉單用醋煮，可留十日。
- 麵不宜生水過，用滾湯停冷，食之。
- 燒肉忌桑柴火。
- 醬蟹、糟蟹忌燈照，則沙。
- 酒酸，用小豆一升，炒焦，袋盛，入酒罈中，則好。
- 染坊瀝過淡灰，晒乾，用以包藏生黃瓜、茄子，至冬月可食。
- 用松毛包藏桔子，三四月不乾。菉豆藏橘，亦可。

---

[59] The word *lian* 蔹 was used, here likely to refer to the harsh and uncomfortable sensations one gets in their mouths eating the unprocessed shoots of certain species of bamboo. The term may have similar origins to the name of the medicinal plant *bailian* 白蔹 (*Ampelopsis japonica*), which supposedly has a strong bitter taste and a sensation on the tongue that some described as "biting" (Taiwanese: *gaga* 咬咬).

[60] Here, the word *lian* 蔹 was used again (See previous use to describe "biting" taste on Page 27) except here in context to rancid oil smells. This makes sense since on top of its oily, sour, or varnish-like smells, rancid oil has a unique mouth feel, with that coat-the-sides-of-your-mouth soapy bite.

吳氏中饋錄

CHAPTER II

PREPARING VEGETABLES
製蔬

Madame Wu's Handbook on Home-Cooking

SALTED GOURD AND BEANS

Take a combined fifty *jin* of old gourds[1] and tender eggplants, for each *jin* use two and a half *liang* of pure salt. First use half a *liang* of salt on the gourds and eggplants to extract their water. Next, combine them together with five *jin* of mandarin peel, three *jin* of fresh perilla [2] with its roots, three *jin* of ginger, two *jin* of peeled apricot kernels, four *liang* of sweet osmanthus flowers, two *liang* licorice, one *dou* of soy beans, and five *jin* of boiled *jiu*. Put them in a wide-mouthed jar, pack them tightly, and cover with five layers of bamboo shoot sheaths. Secure everything with bamboo slats, seal the jar with bamboo shoot sheaths and clay, and then leave it out in the sunlight. After two months, empty the contents and mix it with half a *jin* of Sichuan peppers, and half a *jin* each of fennel and *sharen*. Lay them out evenly to dry in the breeze, until they are warm to the touch and are deliciously tender. For the soy beans, one must choose larger ones. Boil them until soft and cover them under a layer of wheat bran to retain the heat. Remove the bran and clean them before use.

配鹽瓜菽

老瓜、嫩茄合五十斤，每斤用淨鹽二兩半。先用半兩醃瓜、茄一宿，出水。次用橘皮五斤、新紫蘇連根三斤、生薑絲三斤、去皮杏仁二斤、桂花四兩、甘草二兩、黃豆一斗、煮酒五斤，同拌，入瓮，合滿，捺實；箬五層，竹片捺定，箬裹泥封，晒日中。兩月取出，入大椒半斤，茴香、砂仁各半

---

[1] Given that *gua* (瓜) could refer to a wide variety of melon, gourd, or squash from the family *Cucurbitaceae*, it is unclear what is being referred to here. Indeed, then as now, this word could refer to other unrelated fleshy cylindrical fruits, such as the papaya or quince (both known as *mugua* 木瓜). Still considering what is used in modern preserved gourds, the most likely candidates are various cultivars of winter melon or cucumber.

[2] *Perilla frutescens var. Crispa* known as *shiso* 紫蘇 in Japanese.

斤，匀晾晒在日內，發熱，乃酥美。黃豆須揀大者，煮爛，以麩皮罨熱。去麩皮，淨用。

Eggplant steamed with sugar

Take large tender eggplants of the *niuni* variety[3], without removing their heads, cut them axially into six equal segments.[4] For every fifty *jin*, use one *liang* of salt and mix them well. Scald them in water until their colour changes, then let them drip dry. Fill them with powdered mint leaves and fennel, then soak them in a mixture of three *jin* of granulated sugar and half a *zhong* of vinegar for three days. Dry them under the sun, then return them to the soaking liquid, repeating this until the soaking liquid is used up and the eggplants are dried. Press them until flat and store.

糖蒸茄

牛妳茄嫩而大者,不去蒂,直切成六棱。每五十斤用鹽一兩,拌勻,下湯焯,令變色,乾幹。用薄荷、茴香末夾在內,砂糖三斤、醋半鍾浸三宿,晒乾,還滷。直至滷盡茄乾,壓匾,收藏之。

---

[3] The term *niuni* 牛妳, may be a corruption or mistranscription of the term *niunai* 牛奶, which translates as "cow's milk". If true, *nuinique* 牛妳茄 would most likely alludes to the an eggplant variety with bright white skin. While the only modern eggplant variety with a similar name is a Shanghai cultivar (上海牛奶茄, *shanghai niunaiqie*), many white eggplant varieties are still grown in China, including ones that are round and egg-shaped. Looking at these white egg-like eggplant varieties, we immediately understand how the English name for this entire *Solanum* species came to be.

[4] From the descriptions of this recipe, the six segments should remain connected by the head of the eggplant such that they can be filled with the flavouring mixture later.

吳氏中饋錄

STUFFED CUCUMBER

Take a green cucumber that is mature, big, and firm. Slice it into two halves[5], remove the pulp, and rub with salt to extract its water. Slice fresh ginger, dried mandarin peel, mint, and perilla leaves into a thin julienne, and mix evenly with fennel, stir-fried *sharen*, and granulated sugar. Stuff the mix into the gourd and wind thread around it to secure it and make sure it remains whole. Put it into a jar used for soy-paste[6] and remove it after five or six days and dry under the sun. For long-term storage, dry it after chopping into a mince.

釀瓜

青瓜[7]堅老而大者,切作兩片,去穰,略用鹽出其水。生薑、陳皮、薄荷、紫蘇俱切作絲,茴香、炒砂仁、砂糖拌勻,入瓜內,用線扎定成個,入醬缸內。五、六日取出,連瓜晒乾,收貯,切碎了晒。

---

[5]The text specifies as "two slices", which means that the halves should be axial or along the length of the cucumber.

[6]It is unclear from the text whether one needs to place the cucumbers in an empty jar normally used for holding soy-paste or a jar that contains soy-paste.

[7]In modern usage, *qinggua* (青瓜, *lit.* green gourd) refers to cucumber, but considering that text in other parts of this manual distinguishes its use from the term *huanggua* (黃瓜, *lit.* yellow gourd) it poses the question of whether green gourd is indeed cucumber. A guess in this case is that the "green" version is simply the immature and young cucumber commonly found in markets, and the "yellow" version is the fully ripened cucumber fruit with its brownish-yellow crazed and russeted skin. In Li Fang's 李昉 Song dynasty work *Taiping Yulan* 太平御覽, the green gourd was mentioned as being suitable for quenching thirst and reducing fatigue when directly consumed, apparently raw, after being split in half, and alluded as being a common and inexpensive vegetable. It is most plausible that "green gourd" is indeed the green immature cucumber (or a similar species) and thus translated in the recipes as such.

Garlic cucumber

Take a *jin* of autumn harvested cucumber and blanch it in a solution of slaked lime and alum[8], then dry them. Marinade them overnight using half a *liang* of salt. Take another half a *liang* of salt and three *liang* of peeled garlic cloves, pound them into a fine paste, and mix this evenly with the cucumbers. Submerge them, pouring back the marinade liquid, along with good simmered *jiu* and vinegar, then store them in a cool location. Winter melon and eggplant can be similarly prepared.

蒜瓜

秋間小黃瓜一斤，石灰、白礬湯焯過，控幹。鹽半兩醃一宿。又鹽半兩，剝大蒜瓣三兩，搗為泥，與瓜拌勻，傾入醃下水中，熬好酒、醋浸著，涼處頓放，冬瓜、茄子同法。

---

[8] Specifically, potassium alum.

吳氏中饋錄

THRICE-COOKED CUCUMBER

Take green cucumbers that are old and firm, and cut them each into two halves[9]. For each *jin*, marinade them using half a *liang* of salt, one *liang* of soy-paste, and a small amount of both perilla leaves and licorice root. After a day, boil them with their marinade juices during the evening and dry them under the sun during the day, repeating this three times: sun-drying after boiling. Should there be a rainy day, leave them on top of the steaming vessel to steam. After they are fully sun-dried, place them in storage.

三煮瓜

青瓜堅老者切作兩片。每一斤用鹽半兩，醬一兩，紫蘇、甘草少許，醃。伏時連滷，夜煮日晒凡三次。煮後晒。至雨天，留甑上蒸之，晒乾，收貯。

---

[9] Axially, along the length of the cucumber.

DRIED GARLIC SHOOTS

Cut one *jin* of garlic shoots into *cun*-long segments and add one *liang* of salt. Marinate them and extract out their smelly juices. Dry them slightly in the shade, then mix them with soy-paste and a little sugar. Steam them until done, dry them in the breeze, and then store.

蒜苗干

蒜苗切寸段,一斤,鹽一兩。淹出臭水,略晾乾,拌醬、糖少許,蒸熟,晒乾,收藏。

吳氏中饋錄

STORED MUSTARD GREENS

Take plump heads of mustard greens and do not let them touch water. Let them dry under the sun until the are sixty or seventy percent dry, then remove the outer leaves. For each *jin* of mustard, use four *liang* of salt, and marinate them overnight, then remove them. Tie each head into a small bundle and pack them in a small flask. Pour out all the juices and simmer it with the juices produced during marination. Collect only the clear portion of the cooked juice, let it cool, pour it back into the flask, and seal it well.[10] This is eaten during the summer months.

藏芥

芥菜肥者不犯水,晒至六七分乾,去葉。每斤鹽四兩,淹一宿,取出。每莖扎成小把,置小瓶中,倒瀝盡其水。并煎醃出水,同煎。取清汁,待冷,入瓶,封固,夏月食。

---

[10]Except for the step to simmer the briny juice, this recipe is more or less the same as how one would nowadays produce pickled mustard (酸菜, suian cai). On top of this, the packing and sealing of the pickled mustard in flasks is how Hakka *fucai* 福菜 is produced and aged, which may point to how old some of these production methods are.

PIQUANT MUSTARD JUICE

Take mustard seeds[11] that have been aged for two years, grind finely, blend with water, pack it into a bowl, and seal it with tough paper. Put it in boiling water three to five times to extract a yellow liquid then let it cool again on the ground. When pouring out the liquid, one should notice some *qi*.[12] Add mild vinegar to dilute it, and filter it through a cloth to remove any residue.[13]

芥辣

二年陳芥子，碾細，水調，納實椀內，韌紙封固。沸湯三、五次泡出黃水，覆冷地上。傾後有氣，入淡醋解開，布濾去查。

---

[11]TThese are almost certainly the seeds of *Brassica juncea*, with different varieties grown in East Asia for their seeds and their green portions. This is opposed to European mustard seeds, which are more often from *Sinapis alba* (formerly *Brassica alba*).

[12]The term *qi* can describe actual gas, a force, or a scent. While it seems more likely that the word here is used to refer to a sharp smell, it could equally refer to gas from fermentation.

[13]The result is a piquant concentrate extracted from ground mustard seeds, reminiscent of supernatant that forms on top of prepared Dijon mustard.

吳氏中饋錄

Soy-paste Buddha's hand citron, citron, and pear

When placed in a jar of soy-paste, Pears with their skin on will last for a long time without spoiling. For citron[14] remove the pulp and place the peel in soy-paste. For Buddha's hand citron,[15] put the entire fruit in the soy-paste. Fresh mandarin peel, red agar,[16] and wheat gluten can also be preserved in soy-paste to make them taste even better.

醬佛手、香櫞、梨子

梨子帶皮入醬缸內,久而不壞。香櫞去穰,醬皮。佛手全醬。新橘皮、石花、麵筋皆可醬食,其味更佳。

---

[14] *Citrus medica*

[15] *Citrus medica*, var. *sarcodactylis*

[16] "Stone flowers" could either be the terrestrial lichen *Parmelia saxatilis* or the coastal algae *Gelidium amansii*. The latter, sometimes called "red algae" or "agar", is more likely since the former lichens tend not to be used except in small quantities as medicine.

Eggplant in *jiu*-lees

"Five of eggplants, six of lees, and seventeen of salt. Add river water and it turns honey sweet."[17] Meaning, take five *jin* of eggplant, six *jin* of lees, seventeen *liang* of salt, two or three bowls of river water to mix with *jiu*-lees, and the taste of the eggplant will become naturally sweet. This method of preserving eggplant is not for those in haste.

糟茄子法

『五茄六糟鹽十七，更加河水甜如蜜。』茄子五斤，糟六斤，鹽十七兩，河水兩三碗，拌糟，其茄味自甜。此藏茄法也，非暴用者[18]。

---

[17] In Chinese, these rhyming lines are known as *koujue* 口訣. They are a traditional memory aid taught to students to ensure the transmission of knowledge for recipes and techniques, be they for cuisine, medicines, or martial arts.

[18] *Baoyong zhe* 暴用者 translates literally to "one who wants to use something aggressively," which appears to describe someone in a rush. A similar phrase is used in "Radish in *jiu*-lees" on page 42.

吳氏中饋錄

Radish in *jiu*-lees

Take one *jin* of radish and three *liang* of salt. Do not rinse the radishes with water, but rather, wipe them clean. Slice them in half keeping their fines roots and let them sun-dry. Mix the *jiu*-lees with salt, put in a little of the radish, mix everything again and place in a wide-mouthed jar. This method is not for those in a rush to eat them.

糟蘿卜方

蘿蔔一斤,鹽三兩。以蘿蔔不要見水,揩淨,帶須半根晒乾。糟與鹽拌過,少入蘿蔔,又拌過,入甕。此方非暴喫者。

Madame Wu's Handbook on Home-Cooking

GINGER IN *jiu*-LEES

Take one *jin* of ginger, one *jin* of *jiu*-lees, and five *liang* of salt. One can start the pickling before the fiftieth day of Autumn. Do not rinse them with water and do not damage the gingers' skin, rather, wipe off any mud with a dry cloth. Dry them under the sun until half dried, then mix them with the *jiu*-lees and salt mixture and put it into a wide-mouthed jar.

糟薑方

薑一斤,糟一斤,鹽五兩,揀社日[19]前可糟。不要見水,不可損了薑皮,用乾布擦去泥,晒半乾後,糟鹽拌之,入甕。

---

[19] The meaning of the first character, "揀" (*jian*), is unclear, however, *tuanri* 社日 is the 50th day (the 5th *wuri* 戊日) after the first day of either spring (*lichun*, 立春) or autumn (*liqiu*, 立秋). Considering that ginger harvest in central China is typically done during Autumn, one could assume that *jian tuanri* was the 50th day of the Autumn season.

吳氏中饋錄

PREPARING GARLIC SHOOTS

Use somewhat less salt on the shoots, marinate them for one night, and dry them in the breeze. Scald them and lay them out to dry. Mix them with licorice extract, steam them on top of rice steamer, sun-dry, and put them into a wide-mouthed jar.

做蒜苗方

苗用些少鹽,醃一宿,晾幹。湯焯過,又晾幹。以甘草湯拌過,上甑蒸之,晒乾,入甕。

THREE-HARMONIES VEGETABLES

Take one part of mild vinegar, one part of rice *jiu*, one part of water, and season with salt and licorice until the desired taste is achieved. Heat the mixture until it boils, then add a small amount each of slivered vegetable shoots and slivered mandarin peel. Place ones or two small slices of *baizhi* [20] on top of the vegetables, simmer everything in liquid, be sure to not open the lid. When it is done, serve.

三和菜[21]

淡醋一分，酒一分，水一分，鹽、甘草調和其味得所。煎滾，下菜苗絲、橘皮絲各少許，白芷一、二小片摻菜上，重湯頓，勿令開，至熟，食之。

---

[20] *Baizhi* 白芷 are the root portions of *Angelica dahurica*. These are usually sold dried and sliced into medallions.

[21] The fact that there is only one non-descript vegetable listed with a slew of seasonings and spices in this *sanhe cai* recipe makes one wonder whether "Three-harmonies/combined vegetable" is a passable translation. Indeed, due to this uncertainty, the English title for this section has changed five times since the beginning of this translation project. However, Dr. Anderson believes that the name refers to the mix of the three ingredients, water, vinegar, and *jiu* and that the vegetables were then prepared in this mix, hence the name. Considering that these three liquids make up part of the "six beverages" (六飲, *liuyin*) mentioned in the "Rites of Zhou" (周礼, *Zhouli*), perhaps this ternary mix is worthy enough to proclaim as a sort of "harmony", and thus I will leave the title as such.

吳氏中饋錄

QUICK CHOPPED BITS

Take the tender stalks of bok choy[22], scald them in boiling water until half cooked, wring them dry, and chop them into small pieces. Using a little oil, stir-fry them slightly, and put them in a container. Add a little vinegar, wait for a little while and serve.

Take thin red carrots and slice them together with mustard greens. Put them in vinegar and let marinade slightly. When eaten, they are very crisp. Note that one should use a little salt, star anise, fennel, ginger, and mandarin peel slivers, mixed together with vinegar, pickled, then served.

暴虀

菘菜嫩莖,湯焯半熟,紐乾,切作碎段。少加油略炒過,入器內,加醋些少,停少頃,食之

取紅細胡蘿蔔切片,同切芥菜。入醋,略醃片時,食之甚脆,仍用鹽些少,大小茴香、薑、橘皮絲同醋共拌,醃食。

---

[22]The text mentions *song cai* 菘菜, the traditional Chinese medicinal term for the numerous cultivars of *Brassica rapa* var. *chinensis*. The cultivars are also extremely diverse, not only in their form and size, but also in they taste and textures, which range from the various small piquant green mustards to the hefty but mild napa cabbages. Given the relative ambiguity of the type of vegetable in question, I decided to use the English naturalized Cantonese transliteration "bok choy" (白菜, *baicai*), which is use in the modern English langague for describing similar vegetables.

CARROTS PRESERVED IN RED FERMENT STARTER

Cut them into slices, blanch slightly in boiling water, and let them air-dry. Add in a little chopped green onion, star anise and fennel, ginger, slivered mandarin peel, ground Sichuan pepper, red ferment starter, then pulverize them and mixed well with salt. Let marinade[23] a little while and serve.

ANOTHER METHOD

Take white radish, *jiaobai*, and freshly cut bamboo shoots, and boil them until done. These three items can be processed in the same manner to preserve in red ferment starter [24], and they can be eaten together.

胡蘿卜鮓

切作片子，滾湯略焯，控乾。入少許蔥花、大小茴香、薑、橘絲、花椒末、紅麴，研爛同鹽拌勻，罨一時，食之。

又方

白蘿蔔、茭白、生切笋，煮熟。三物俱同比法作鮓，可供食。

---

[23] It is interesting to see both character for of marinade/pickling "罨" and "醃" (*yan*) used in the Chinese. Perhaps the former is for general pickling, while the latter with its *jiu* radical actually indicates its use with alcohol or vinegar?

[24] The Chinese text simply indicates "...to make *zha* 鮓", which is to pickle the ingredient in red ferment starter.

吳氏中饋錄

Garlic greens

Use pale and tender garlic greens and chop them into *cun* long segments. For every ten *jin*, use four *liang* of toasted salt. For each,[25] use one bowl of vinegar and two bowls of water, and soak them inside a wide-mouthed jar.

蒜菜

用嫩白蒜菜切寸段,每十斤用炒鹽四兩,每醋一碗、水二碗,浸菜於瓮內。

---

[25]The "each" here likely refers to each *jin* of the garlic greens.

MAKING PLAIN DRIED EGGPLANT

Take a large eggplant, wash it clean, and boil it in the pot. Do not rinse it afterwards.[26] Split it open and press it with a stone until dry. On the next sunny day, place a tile under the sunlight until it is hot, then spread the eggplant on the tile until sufficiently dry. Store it until the first or second month of the year, and prepare food with it. Its flavours will be like that of fresh eggplants.[27]

淡茄乾方

用大茄洗淨,鍋內煮過,不要見水。擘開,用石壓乾。趁日色晴,先把瓦晒熱,攤茄子於瓦上,以乾為度。藏至正二月內,和物勻,食其味如新茄之味。

---

[26]Throughout the text, the author advises us not to rinse the ingredients that are being processed for picking or preservation. The reason behind this advice is likely because using untreated "raw" water for washing and rinsing may introduce microorganisms that will cause the preserved food to go bad during prolonged storage. This concern is especially valid for this recipe where the eggplants are preserved without salt and thus more prone to spoilage if extra care is not taken to keep them away from possible contaminants.

[27]I was skeptical the first time I read this. After all, this eggplant was dried months earlier and must be reconstituted before eating, which severely limits how fresh tasting it could be. But considering that in an age without greenhouses and intercontinental transportation, one would be so desperate for fresh vegetables by the early month of the year that anything remotely resembling unsalted or unpickled eggplant would seem new and absolutely delicious. Even in the Qing dynasty, Yuan Mei in the *Suiyuan Shidan* said specifically that when one finds preserved vegetables out of season, "...even such a typically worthless food becomes a precious item" [8, p.35 (須知單:時節須知)].

吳氏中饋錄

Soy-paste pickled cucumber

Take one *jin* of "yellow grain",[28] one *jin* of cucumber, and four *liang* of salt. Wipe the cucumber of the marinade liquid coming from it, and mix the yellow paste well. Put it out on plate twice a day [29] for a period of "seven-seven-forty-nine"[30] days, then put everything in a wide-mouthed jar.

盤醬瓜茄法[31]

黃子一斤,瓜一斤,鹽四兩。將瓜擦原醃瓜水,拌勻醬黃,每日盤二次,七七四十九日入罈。

---

[28] This preserved cucumber dish is likely something similar to a cucumber *misozuke* 味噌漬け.

[29] The literal translation here, and in the previous sentence, may sound somewhat cryptic, but it simply instructs one on how to even out the "yellow grain" pickling paste. Specifically, you take the cucumbers out of the paste, rid them of any excess liquids, put them on a clean plate, mix the paste until even, then pack the cucumbers back into the paste. Although not wholly related, this reminds me of making Japanese *kasuzuke* 糠漬け, where maintaining the rice bran pickling bed's evenness and moisture content is critical.

[30] It is interesting to see this phrase used here, considering that it is from the Buddhist belief that the spirit of the dead takes forty-nine days to pass through a series of trials to reach the heavens or be banished to hell. Colloquially, it is used to describe a task requiring a prolonged period of work and effort. Either the author was a devout Buddhist and took religion into her culinary duties, or more likely, this term has already been secularized by the late Song dynasty.

[31] The literal translation for this dish is "Dished cucumbers pickled in soy-paste in the manner of eggplants". The name has been simplified, not least for legibility but also because the eggplants mentioned in the name do not appear in the recipe.

DRIED GREENS IN SEALED-JARS

Take ten *jin* of greens, toast forty two *liang* of salt, and use a large jar to pickle the green, with a layer of greens then a layer of salt. Pickle them for three days, then retrieve them. Place the greens on a dish and knead them once, then place them in another large jar. Reserve the salt brine for later use. After another three days, retrieve the greens again and knead them again, place them in yet another large jar, and reserve the salty brine for later use. When this has been done nine times over, put the greens inside a wide-mouthed jar. Arrange the greens thus: for every layer of greens, sprinkle on a layer of Sichuan pepper and fennel, and repeat with more greens. Pack them tightly, then for each jar pour in three bowls of the previously reserved salty brine. Seal them with clay and eat them during the New Year.

乾閉瓮菜

菜十斤,炒鹽四十兩,用缸醃菜。一皮菜,一皮鹽,醃三日,取起。菜入盆內,揉一次,將另過一缸,鹽滷收起聽用。又過三日,又將菜取起,又揉一次,將菜另過一缸,留鹽汁聽用。如此九遍完,入瓮內。一層菜上,洒花椒、小茴香一層,又裝菜如此。緊緊實實裝好,將前留起菜滷,每罈澆三碗,泥起,過年可吃。

吳氏中饋錄

Tossed mixed greens

Add sesame oil to Sichuan pepper, simmer it for one or two *gun* then put it away. When one is ready to use it, pour the oil into a bowl, add a small amount of soy-sauce, vinegar, and white sugar. Blend it together well and reserve. For any food that one wishes to toss with the oil, quickly pour on a small amount, then toss and serve it for a good dish. If you wish to toss it with bok choy, bean sprouts, or watercress, you must first blanch the greens in boiling water until done, then immerse it in clean water to soak. When ready, wring it dry, toss it with the oil, and serve. Done thus, the greens will retain their bright emerald colour, will not turn dark, and remain crisp and delicious.

撒拌和菜

將麻油入花椒,先時熬一、二滾,收起。臨用時,將油倒一碗,入醬油、醋、白糖些少,調和得法安起。凡物用油拌的,即倒上些少,拌吃絕妙。如拌白菜、豆芽、水芹,須將菜入滾水焯熟,入清水漂著。臨用時榨乾,拌油方吃。菜色青翠,不黑,又脆,可口。

STEAMED DRIED VEGETABLE

Choose a large, good quality vegetable and wash it well, then put it directly into boiling water. Blanch until it is fifty or sixty percent cooked, then dry it under the sun. Next cook it with salt, soy-paste, dill,[32] Sichuan pepper, granulated sugar, mandarin peel until it has completely cooked through. Sun-dry it again then steam quickly while place sealed in a porcelain container. When serving, douse it with "fragrant oil" and knead it together quickly, and add a little vinegar. Steam it on top of rice then serve.

蒸乾菜

將大窠好菜擇洗净，乾入沸湯內，焯五六分熟，晒乾。用鹽、醬、蒔蘿、花椒、砂糖、橘皮同煮，極熟；又晒乾，并蒸片時，以磁器收貯，用時着香油沖揉，微用醋。飯上蒸食。

---

[32] Considering that the rest of the ingredients here are dry or preserved, the dill used is likely dill seed.

吳氏中饋錄

Quail eggplants

Choose a tender eggplant and slice it into fine slivers, blanch in boiling water, and air-dry. Grind salt, soy-paste, Sichuan pepper, dill, fennel, licorice, dried mandarin peel, apricot kernels, and azuki beans into a fine powder. Mix everything together well, sun dry, and steam, before reserving it for later use. To serve, soak it until soft with boiling water, shallow fry in "fragrant oil".[33]

鵪鶉茄[34]

揀嫩茄切作細縷,沸湯焯過,控乾。用鹽、醬、花椒、蒔蘿、茴香、甘草、陳皮、杏仁、紅豆研細末,拌勻,晒乾,蒸過收之。用時以滾湯泡軟,蘸香油煠之。

---

[33]The soaking and frying were likely done with the whole mass of the eggplant mixture together rather than breaking it up. Regarding the frying process, the text tells us to "adhere it to fragrant oil and fry". In this case, the "adhere" may indicate that only the surface of the mass of eggplant is fried, thus producing a crispy crust (similar to how someone would pan-fry a whole bird).

[34]The dish likely gets its name from the similarity of appearance to the feather patterns of the Japanese Quail (*Coturnix japonica*). The thin slivers of eggplant mixed with its flavouring powder and pan-fried, would make it brownish and beige, punctuated with a long whitish lines, which would resemble the brown spiked pattern on the bird's feathers. While the name could also indicate the similarity of flavour of this dish to actual quail, it would take some imagination.

SHIXIANG EGGPLANTS

Cut as many eggplants[35] as desired into game-piece[36] sized rounds. Use eight *qian* of salt per *jin*. Mix the *shixiang*[37] well with the eggplants, pickle them in a large jar for one or two days, then retrieve and air dry them. During the daytime, sun-dry them, and in the evening, return them to the brine. Retrieve them and sun-dry them again the next day, and do this three times, but do not over-dry them. Store them in a wide-mouthed jar for use.

---

[35] The type of eggplant specified here is called "gourd eggplant" (*guaqie* 瓜茄), which likely refers to a specific variety with a gourd-like form.

[36] Specifically, the thick disk-shape of *xiangqi* 象棋 game pieces.

[37] A quick survey of works from the Yuan to the Qing dynasty (See footnote 38), tell us that *shixiang* (食香 or 十香) here likely refers to a herb and spice mixture. However, it should also be noted that *shixiangcai* 十香菜, is a colloquial name for spearmint *Mentha spicata* in some parts of central China.

吳氏中饋錄

食香瓜茄[38]

不拘多少,切作棊子,每斤用鹽八錢,食香同瓜拌勻,於缸內醃一、二日取出,控乾。日晒,晚複入滷水內,次日又取出晒,凡經三次。勿令太乾,裝入罈內用。

---

[38] This pickled and preserved eggplant dish appears well-liked enough to be transmitted in one form or another into the Qing dynasty. This recipe (and many others from this book) was copied in facsimile in the Ming dynasty lifestyle compendium the *Zunsheng Bajian* 遵生八箋 and mentioned in the Ming dynasty erotic novel *Jinpingmei* 金瓶梅. The Yuan dynasty "Omnibus of Household Essentials" (*Jujiabiyoung Shilei Quanji*, 居家必用事类全集) provided a somewhat related recipe for *Shixiang Qie'er* 食香茄兒 also with salted dried preserved eggplant but flavoured with slivered ginger, mandarin peel, perilla leaves, sugar, and vinegar. A very similar recipe in the Qing dynasty compendium *Wuli Xiaoshi* 物理小識 for *Shixiang Guashi* (十香瓜豉) prepares the dried eggplants with a soy-paste starter culture but flavoured with cassia cinnamon, galangal, slivered ginger, mandarin peel, fennel, Sichuan pepper, perilla leaf, mint, and fresh rice *jiu*. More distantly related, the Qing dynasty novel "Dream of the Red Pavilion", recounted an even more elaborate and extravagant preparation for pickled, dried eggplant known as *qiexiang* (茄鯗, lit. eggplant in the style of dried fish).

Madame Wu's Handbook on Home-Cooking

Jiu-LEES EGGPLANT

For every five *jin* of eggplant, use ten *liang* of salt, and mix them together with *jiu*-lees. Take fifty wens worth of copper coins, and arrange them on top of the pickles. Removed the coins after ten days and put them away. Next, replace the *jiu*-lees and put them in a flask. Even after prolonged storage, their colour will remain emerald green as if they were brand new.[39]

糟瓜茄

瓜茄等物每五斤,鹽十兩,和糟拌勻。用銅錢五十文逐層鋪上,經十日取錢,不用。另換糟入瓶。收久,翠色如新。

---

[39] Some interesting Song dynasty applications of inorganic chemistry to food preparation, arguably to the health detriment of whoever consumed too much of the end product. Here, the application of the predominantly copper coins in the pickling eggplants resulted in the formation of copper salts that gave the pickles their vibrant blue-green colour. These copper salts were also likely antimicrobial and pesticidal to some extent, which would have aided in preservation. The coins were alloyed with lead and tin in relatively high proportions, so these metal salts would have also been part of this mixture. Combined with acetic acid from the continuous oxidation of the *jiu*-lees, this would have formed some lead acetate, which may have given the pickles a hint of the toxic sweet taste that the Romans adored.

吳氏中饋錄

Jiaobai PRESERVED IN RED FERMENT STARTER

Slice the *jiaobai*, blanch, and air dry them. Pound slivered green onion, dill, fennel, Sichuan pepper, and red ferment starter into a paste, then mix well with salt. Marinade everything together for a while and serve. Lotus shoots pickled in red ferment starter[40] are also prepared in the same manner.

茭白鮓[41]

鮮茭切作片子,焯過,控乾。以細葱絲、蒔蘿、茴香、花椒、紅麴研爛,并鹽拌勻,同醃一時,食。藕梢鮓同此造法。

---

[40] From the late spring to summer, the dormant lotus roots (technically rhizomes) will continually push shoots through the lake mud to extend their reach to the water's surface to grow leaves. Typically, only the leaf shoots are harvested for consumption as a vegetable. When done before they reach sunlight, they will remain milky white and tender. Like the lotus rhizomes, these shoots are similarly hollow, with long tunnels that function as the plant's complex internal respiratory/gas exchange system extending the entire lengths of the shoots.

[41] It should be noted that a very similar recipe for this is found in the Yuan dynasty "Omnibus of Household Essentials" (居家必用事类全集, *jujiabiyung shileiquanji*), which provides more details on the preparation of this pickled dish. A plainer variant of this can also be found in Yuan Mei's Qing dynasty *Suiyuan Shidan* (隨園食單).

Sweet and sour eggplant

Take tender new eggplant and cut them into triangular blocks,[42] then pour boiling water over them while in a strainer.[43] Wrap them in a cloth and wring them dry, and salt them for one night. Dry them under the sun, mix well with slivered ginger and perilla leaves, then simmer them with sugar and vinegar until the liquid bubbles and everything has been absorbed. Store in a porcelain container. Gourds can be prepared in the same manner.

糖醋茄

取新嫩茄切三角塊，沸湯漉過，布包榨乾，鹽淹一宿。晒乾，用薑絲、紫蘇拌匀，煎滾糖醋潑浸，收入磁器內。瓜同此法。

---

[42]These triangular blocks are either cut by a large "rolling-blade" or diagonal cuts, which produces pyramidal or wedge-like prisms respectively.

[43]The text translates literally to "strained through boiling water", which should be interpreted as pouring boiling water over the raw eggplants while everything is in a strainer.

吳氏中饋錄

Garlic winter melon

Pick the larger specimens, peel them, and discard their seed and pulp. Blanch them in boiling water with alum and slaked-lime, strain, and air-dry them. For every *jin*, pound two *liang* of salt and three *liang* of garlic cloves into a paste, then fill them into a porcelain vessel with the winter melon. Fill it with good vinegar that has been simmered[44] and allow everything to soak.

蒜冬瓜

揀大者去皮穰，切如一指濶。以白礬、石灰煎湯焯過，漉出，控乾。每斤用鹽二兩，蒜瓣三兩，搗碎，同冬瓜裝入磁器，添以熬過好醋，浸之。

---

[44]This may have be done to pasteurize the vinegar or its vinegar culture or to rid it of some of its odours.

CURING SALTED GARLIC CHIVES

Before the frost, pick garlic chives that are plump without yellow leaves. Clean by picking through them, then wash and air dry. Spread a layer of garlic chives in the porcelain pot, followed by sprinkling a layer of salt, then after the salt another layer of garlic chives and do so until everything is used up. Pickle for one or two nights, turning them over several times, then put them into a porcelain vessel. Serve with the chive's pickling liquid, adding a little "fragrant oil" for something quite wonderful.[45]

醃鹽韭法

霜前，揀肥韭無黃梢者，擇淨，洗，控乾。於磁盆內鋪韭一層，糝鹽一層，候鹽、韭勻鋪，盡為度，醃一、二宿，翻數次，裝入磁器內。用原滷加香油少許，尤妙。

---

[45] Pickled garlic chives (*yanjiucai* 腌韭菜) are still prepared and eaten in the same manner in modern times, served with its pickling juices and drizzled with sesame oil. It seems some things do not change much, even over centuries.

吳氏中饋錄

MAKING *gu* GREENS

Use choy sum[46] during spring that has not become old and tough. Remove all their leaves, wash them, and chop them into small dice as large as the centre of coins.[47] Sun-dry until they are no longer damp, but do not let them become too dry. Stir-fry them with slivered ginger and processed soy beans.[48] Use one *liang* of salt one for every *jin*, add *shixiang*,[49] and let it rest. Knead any salty juices back into the greens and store them in a large jar. Use when it has ripened.

造穀菜[50]法

用春不老菜臺,去葉,洗淨,切碎,如錢眼子大。晒乾水氣,勿令太乾,以薑絲炒,黃豆大,每菜一斤,用鹽一兩,入食香,相停揉回滷性,裝入礶內,候熟隨用。

---

[46]The text asked for *caitai* 菜苔, which is a large stem cultivar of *Brassica rapa*, the common oil-seed mustard. Of all the typical present-day varieties, the "*choysum/caixin*" 菜心 variety *Brassica rapa* subsp. *parachinensis* is likely the most similar due to its fine textured and large crisp stem. As with many other varieties of this species, it stands up well to light frost and can be grown even during winter in milder climates.

[47]The coins of the Southern Song dynasty have a square hole of around 8mm squared, making these 8mm dice.

[48]The Chinese text could be translated literally as "great yellow beans" (*huangdou da* 黃豆大), which could be understood as being rather large specimens of soybean or soaked soybeans (thus becoming large). These could have also been soybeans that have been cured and fermented. Due to the ambiguity, it is translated here as "processed soybeans".

[49]See Shixiang eggplants on page 55

[50]*Gucai* (穀菜/榖菜) *Solanum lyratum*, more commonly known in Chinese as *baiying* (白英), is a medicinal plant used in traditional Chinese medicine and considered mildly poisonous. This is unsurprising considering that it is of the nightshade family, and its poisonous traits have not been completely bred out via domestication for its medicinal qualities. Why this preparation was named as such is unclear, considering it does not involve any *baiying*. The name of this dish may have originated from a recipe that initially used the poisonous solanum plant, which later cooks substituted for a more palatable and safe mustard green.

Napa cabbage

Cut the leaves off the napa cabbage stalk,[51] leaving only the heart of the cabbage, which should be two *cun* from its flattened fertilized soil. Cover it with a large jar and seal it on the outside thoroughly with soil. Do not allow any air to enter. After half a month, it is ready to harvest and serve, when its flavour will be at its best.[52]

黃芽菜

將白菜割去梗葉，止留菜心，離地二寸許，以糞土壅平，用大缸覆之。缸外以土密壅，勿令透氣，半月後取食，其味最佳。

---

[51] The unfurled leaves growing off the main stalk around the tightly packed head of napa cabbage must be removed.

[52] A delightful, if not somewhat unusual, horticultural technique for growing tasty napa cabbage.

吳氏中饋錄

Inverted Greens

For every hundred pounds of greens, use fifty *liang* of salt. Place them in a wide-mouthed jar to pickle, packing them tight. Mix hair and ash[53] together with salt brine to the consistency of a dry wheat dough. Apply it over the jar's opening, spread it, and seal well. One does not need to stop it first with grass.[54]

Use mustard greens, do not rinse them with water, and let them dry in the breeze. When they are limp, quickly blanch them in boiling water, remove them using a strainer, then let them cool in the breeze on a sieve. Cool off the liquid used to blanch the mustard greens. Sprinkle and mix the vegetables in the sieve with a little loose salt and fill them into a flask. Pour the cooled vegetables blanching liquid[55] on top of them, wrap well, and set them undisturbed over cold ground.[56]

---

[53] Medical texts such as the *Tang Bencao* 唐本草 and the *Bencao Shiyi* 本草拾遺 indicate that *maohui* 毛灰 is ash made from burning feather, hair, or skin. Such ash derived from different animals and hairs of various hues is purported to have different medical properties and indications. Still, any attempts at using this medical ingredient in the manner described here as a sealant would have been unfruitful since it could not have provided any actual structure or adhesive properties. The more likely reading here should be "hair and stone ash", a reinforced cement mixture of hair mixed with slaked lime.

[54] Because the sealing cement described here contains animal hair, it has enough tensile strength to bridge over the container's opening without first stopping the container with grass to provide structural support.

[55] The text asks for the cooled vegetable brine (*lu* 滷). However, we see that neither the boiling liquid nor the vegetables was salted.

[56] This recipe reads like two different recipes, with the latter more complete than the former. Perhaps this is an old transcription error, which accidentally glommed two unrelated recipes together over the centuries.

Madame Wu's Handbook on Home-Cooking

倒蠹菜[57]

每菜一百斤,用鹽五十兩,醃入了罈,裝實,用鹽滷調毛灰如乾麵糊口上,攤過封好,不必草塞。

用芥菜,不要落水晾乾。軟了,用滾湯一焯就起,笊籬撈,在篩子內晾冷,將焯菜湯晾冷。將篩子內菜用鬆鹽些少撒拌,入瓶後,加晾冷菜滷淙上,包好,安頓冷地上。

---

[57] The recipe name is difficult to elucidate due to the complicated second character. Transcribed here as *dao* 蠹, it means "military streamer/banner", which is mostly meaningless when used in this context. Several modern transcriptions replace it with the morphologically dissimilar "菹" (*zu*, lit. to pickled vegetables), which feels like a translation cop-out since it basically disposes of the original character and arbitrarily chooses one that happens describe the techniques used in the recipes. The Ming dynasty edition of the *Shuo Fu* 說郛 anthology, which this publication is based, appears to use either "蠹" or a slightly different character made up of the vertically combined characters "毒" (*du*, lit. poisonous) and "絲" (*si*, lit. filament/silk) but considering the age and print quality of the edition, it is hard to tell. A haphazard guess on how this came about would be that it was the vertical concatenation of two different characters resulting from an ancient mistranscription. If we chose to split this character into two, it would either make or *qingxian* (青縣, lit. green county) or *qingsi* (青絲, lit. green filaments), respectively. Although "inverted green county vegetables" or "inverted green filament vegetables" make much more sense, these readings are still far from satisfactory or concrete. Given that a good recipe name translation is impossible due to the ambiguity and lack of good information, I chose not to translate the character. Instead, I skipped over it, thus resulting in this somewhat awkward English recipe name. So yes, in many ways, this recipe name ended up being somewhat of a cop-out as well.

吳氏中饋錄

Dried bamboo shoots

Take tender bamboo shoots during the spring, peel them well and remove any tough tips. Cut them into pieces that are four *fen* wide and one *cun* long, then steam them in a steamer until cooked. Wrap them in cloth and wring them until they are very dry. Then put them in a storage vessel. Serve prepared in oil.[58] This is also the same method for making dried gluten.

筍鮓

春間取嫩笋,剝淨,去老頭,切作四分大、一寸長塊,上籠蒸熟,以布包裹,榨作極乾,投於器中,下油用。製造與麩鮓同。

---

[58] This part could be read as "served cooked in oil" or "serve with oil." Either way, this may very well be the Song dynasty equivalent of "bamboo shoots braised in oil" (油燜筍絲, *youmensunsi*))

Mild sun-dried bamboo shoots

Get fresh bamboo shoots with tips that look like cat ears, using as much as one desires. Peel them, cut them into long slices, and blanch them in boiling water. Let them dry in the breeze, and store them. To use, soak them until soft in water from rinsing rice. Their colour will become is white as silver. When blanched in boiling brine, they are essentially pickled bamboo shoots.

晒淡笋乾

鮮笋貓耳頭,不拘多少,去皮,切片條,沸湯焯過,晒乾,收貯。用時,米泔水浸軟,色白如銀,鹽湯焯,即醃筍矣。

吳氏中饋錄

Making *jiu douchi*

Take one *dou* and five *sheng* of "yellow grains" that have been sieved until clean of any loose powder[59], five *jin* of eggplants, twelve *jin* of cucumbers, fourteen *liang* of shredded ginger,[60] slivered mandarin peel as desired, one *sheng* of fennel, four *jin* six *liang* of toasted salt, and a *jin* of green Sichuan pepper, all mixed and placed into a large jar, then packed tight. Pour in "golden flower" *jiu* or fresh brewed *jiu*, until it covers everything by two *cun*. Wrap and bind the container with paper and bamboo slats. Seal it with clay, and leave it outside for forty-nine days. On top of the jar, write the words "East" and "West" and expose each side to the sun in turn. Pour the contents into a large basin, sun-dry them sufficiently, and cover them with a yellow grass mat.

酒豆豉方

黃子一斗五升，篩去麵，令淨，茄五斤，瓜十二斤，薑觔十四兩，桔絲隨放，小茴香一升、炒鹽四斤六兩、青椒一斤，一處拌入瓮中，捺實，傾金花酒或酒娘，醃過各物兩寸。許(紙)箬扎縛，泥封，露四十九日。罈上寫「東」、「西」字記號，輪晒日滿，傾大盆內，晒乾為度，以黃草布罩蓋。

---

[59] I translated this as "powder", even though the original character used here was *mian* 麵, which would translate to "wheat flour". The reason is that the ambiguously named "yellow grain" was most likely a mould-based fermentation starter, and what was being sieved out was likely the powdery mould spores and not any real wheat flour.

[60] This original text could be translated as "fourteen *liang* of ginger tendons". More likely, though, this was originally "fourteen *liang* of shredded ginger" and the character *jin* (觔) was a mistranscription of slivers/shred (絲, si), and it should have been "薑絲十四兩". This interpretation was informed in large part by the fact that the recipe following this for Water *douchi* (Page 69) mentions the use of ginger in shredded form. While "ginger and tendon" (薑觔) exists as a modern dish eaten during the colder months of the year, if it existed back in the Song dynasty, it would still have been an unlikely ingredient to be used for pickling.

Madame Wu's Handbook on Home-Cooking

WATER *douchi*

Take ten *jin* of good "yellow grain", forty *liang* of good salt, and ten bowls of Jinhua sweet *jiu*. On the day before, use twenty bowls of boiling water to fully dissolve the salt and make a brine, let it cool and settle until clear, and reserve for use. Put the "yellow grain" into a large jar, add the *jiu* and the salt water, and let it bask under the sun for forty-nine days until done. Add one *liang* each of star anise and fennel, five *qian* of black cardamom, five *qian* of high grade cassia, three *qian* of costus,[61] one *liang* of shredded mandarin peel, one *liang* of Sichuan pepper, half a *jin* of dried shredded ginger, one *jin* of apricot kernels, and place all the ingredients into the large jar. After two days of basking it under the sun with vigorously stirring, put it into a large jar. It is best eaten the following year. It is excellent eaten as a dip for meat.[62]

水豆豉法

好黃子十斤,好鹽四十兩,金華甜酒十碗。先日,用滾湯二十碗,衝充調鹽作滷,留冷,淀清,聽用。將黃子下缸,入酒,入鹽水,晒四十九日,完。方下大小茴香各一兩、草果五錢、官桂五錢、木香三錢、陳皮絲一兩、花椒一兩、乾薑絲半斤、杏仁一斤,各料和入缸內,又晒又打二日,將罈裝起。隔來年吃,方好。蘸肉吃,更妙。

---

[61] The root of the costus plant *Saussurea costus*

[62] The production techniques described here show this is a well-spiced, unfiltered soy-sauce. Short of the spices, this combination of mould-cultured soybeans, brine, and sometimes *jiu* is still how soy-sauce is made in many East Asian areas. Looking at this recipe and the previous one (See Making *jiu douchi* on Page 68), and also knowing how their solids will sink to reveal a dark, clear liquid at the top, one could arguably point to these are the direct predecessors of modern soy-sauce.

吳氏中饋錄

Red salt beans

First take one salt frost ume[63] and press it onto the bottom of the pot. Rinse large black soy beans[64] until clean and cover the ume with it. Form the mound of beans into a nest with a hollow in the middle then add salt into it. Simmer sappanwood[65] in water and add a small amount of alum. Pour this down along all four sides of the pot until it just covers the beans. Simmer until dry, with the beans are thoroughly cooked through, the salt solution is no longer visible, and everything has turned reddish.[66]

---

[63] According to the *Bencao Gangmu* 本草綱目, frost ume (*shuangmei* 霜梅) is also known as salt ume (*yanmei* 鹽梅) or white ume (白梅, baimei). Of the latter, the *Qimin Yaoshu* 齊民要術 provided a recipe, which involved harvesting unripe green ume, repeatedly soaking them in brine and drying them in full sunlight, then packing them in a vessel to let them cure and ripen.

[64] The literal translation here is "large grained blue-green beans" (大粒青豆), which by examining the recipe we can be quite certain were actually black soybeans (*Glycine max*). There were no lack of beans to choose from within Chinese cuisine, but only two common beans that fit within the range of hues specified by the colour "*qing*" 青, specifically, the greenish mung bean (*Vigna radiata*) and the black soybean. But even in the Song dynasty, the former was almost always referred to as "green bean" (綠豆, ludou). Furthermore, due to the high anthocyanin content of black soybean seed coats, when acidic ingredients are mixed in, the dark reddish brown colour of the cooked beans transform to a dull red colour. Since the black soybean is likely the only reasonable "*qing*" coloured bean in Chinese cuisine to fit in this context, we translate directly thus.

[65] An ingredient in Chinese herbology, derived from the woody branches of the leguminous tropical tree *Biancaea sappan*.

[66] The simmering of black soybeans with the acidic ume and potassium alum solution causes their anthocyanins to ionize to a darker red colour, thus producing red beans. The process is chemically similar to adding vinegar to red cabbage water, which takes the solution's colour from a purple-blue to a bright red.

紅鹽豆

先將鹽霜梅一個安在鍋底下,淘淨大粒青豆、蓋梅。又將豆中作一窩,下鹽在內。用蘇木煎水入白礬些少,沿鍋四邊澆下,平豆為度。用火燒乾,豆熟,鹽又不泛而紅。

吳氏中饋錄

Garlic ume

Take two *jin* of hard green ume, one *jin* of garlic, all peeled clean in a bag,[67] and toast three *liang* of salt. Simmer everything in an appropriate quantity of water, let cool, and let them soak. After fifty days, the brine will have changed colour. Pour it away, and simmer them again in water, let cool, soak, and fill them into a flask. Eat them after July.[68] The ume will no longer have a sour taste, and the garlic will no longer have any pungency.

蒜梅

青硬梅子二斤,大蒜一斤,或囊剝淨,炒鹽三兩,酌量水煎湯,停冷,浸之。候五十日後,滷水將變色,傾出,再煎其水,停冷,浸之入瓶。至七月後食,梅無酸味,蒜無葷氣也。

---

[67] The Chinese text here says "...or sack peeled clean" (或囊剝淨), which I assume means that a bag was used to peel clean all the garlic cloves used in this recipe.

[68] This means that ume were preserved right when harvested in spring and ready to eat in the middle of summer after only two months of aging.

Chapter III

Sweet Foods
甜食

MAKING TOASTED WHEAT FLOUR

Sift white flour three times, repeatedly. Place it into a big pot and stir with a wooden implement[1] until it is very well toasted. Place it on a table and pound and crush with an old roller[2] until it is fine, then sift it again. Store it to make sweet food. If one uses butter, it must be fresh, if it has become old, it should not be used.[3]

炒麵方

白麵要重羅三次,將入大鍋內,以木爬炒得大熟,上桌古轤槌碾細,再羅一次,方好做甜食。凡用酥油,須要新鮮,如陳了,不堪用矣。

---

[1]The Chinese term here is *mupa* 木爬, which translates literally to "wooden climb". This most likely refers to a dull, flattened wooden paddle similar to a *mupa* 木扒, which is still commonly used for stirring and cooking large quantities of food.

[2]The text translates literally to: "...place on table and use an old pulley reel to pound and crush them until fine". It is hard to say what this pulley reel looked like and how someone was meant to use it. Perhaps it was something to be held like a rolling pin or rolled like those large pivoting stone wheels traditionally used for crushing olive fruits in the Mediterranean.

[3]Toasted wheat flour is still an essential food item in many parts of Asia and is used to make everything from the sweet or savoury *miancha* 麵茶 consumed in various parts of China and Taiwan to the buttery *tsampa* of Tibet and Central Asia.

吳氏中饋錄

Flour halva

Take any small pot, it doesn't matter how many *jin* or *liang* it is. Put in two ladles of sugar syrup. Add any quantity of butter into the small pot. The butter must be already heated well and filtered clean with a fine cloth.[4] Take plain flour and add to it by hand such that the mixture is neither too thin nor too thick. Toast this mix with a small implement, until the flour is well done. First, simmer the sugar syrup until it you can see fine sugar floss when you dip and lift a stick out of it, then it can be completely poured into the pot containing the butter and flour mixture. Beat everything until it is even, then take it out of the pot. While it is still hot, spread it by over a flat surface[5], roll it out, and cut it into "elephant eye" pieces[6].

麵和油法[7]

不拘斤兩用小鍋，糖滷用二杓，隨意多少酥油下小鍋，煎過，細布濾淨。用生麵隨手下，不稀不稠，用小爬兒炒，至麵熟方好。先將糖滷熬得有絲，棍蘸起視之，可斟酌傾入油麵鍋內。打勻，撥起鍋，乘熱撥在案上，捍開，切象眼塊。

---

[4] This recipe makes used of clarified butter and specifies how it is prepared here.

[5] The flat surface here is a *han* 案, which referred to a large rectangular table top during the Tang dynasty. In earlier times, it referred to a wooden platter supported by short legs, which in some ways was just another kind of low table.

[6] A literal translation of the term, what it is is actually describing a large rhomboid prism form. In Western terms, these are "lozenges".

[7] The Chinese recipe name says "technique for preparing flour combined with fat" (麵和油法). But since we know this is flour halva, we might as well just call it that. The methods for preparing this, from making the butter and flour roux, the way the consistency of the sugar syrup is tested, all the way to the actual shape of the finished pastry, is almost exactly like making South Asian *sooji* or semolina *barfi*.

Madame Wu's Handbook on Home-Cooking

SNOWFLAKE PASTRIES

Put fat into a small pot, melt it, and filter it. Add in handfuls of toasted flour[8], and mix. The mixture should neither be too thin nor thick. Remove from the flames. Sprinkle pure white sugar powder into the toasted flour mixture and stir well until well combined. Place it onto a flat surface, roll it out, and cut into "elephant eye" pieces.[9][10]

雪花酥[11]

油下小鍋化開,濾過,將炒麵隨手下,攪勻,不稀不稠,掇離火。洒白糖末,下在炒麵內,攪勻,和成一處。上案,捍開,切象眼塊。

---

[8] See Making toasted wheat flour on Page 75.

[9] This is a large rhombus shape. Also known as a "lozenge", this is the traditional shape for many types of Central and South Asian semolina halva desserts.

[10] This is another type of halva somewhat similar to Flour halva on Page 76, except a rather finely ground powdered sugar is used instead of sugar syrup. I have tried this recipe a few times, and its dry but paradoxically melt-in-your-mouth texture reminded me of South Asian *nankhatai* or Persian *nan-e nokhodchi*, which was made in a similar fashion but with chickpea.

[11] Although the name may refer to the colour and fine texture of the finished pastries, I suspect it may also refer to the cooling sensation one experiences on the tongue when eating this pastry caused by the large amounts of fat and powdered sugar. The cooling properties of dissolving powdered sugar and melting solid fats are well-known and commonly experienced when eating donuts with powdered sugar. This effect is also central to a class of Western confection known in German as *ischoklad*, which combines large quantities of powdered sucrose or glucose along with low melting-point butter fat, coconut oil, or cocoa butter to produce a cooling sensation as the confection rapidly melts and dissolves in the mouth. Made mainly in the winter due to how badly it keeps in the heat, this confection is available in North America as "Moritz Icy Squares". It is also the key component in making Japanese candymaker Meiji's "Meltykiss" products "melty".

吳氏中饋錄

Making *Saboni*

Simmer using ingredients for simmering *megu*[12] until done. Do not use walnuts. Ladle it out on a flat surface and spread it out. Surround and hold it in with glutinous rice flour,[13] and stamp out pieces using a copper ring. This is "saboni". If cut in the form of elephant tusks,[14] they are known as "white sugar pieces".

---

[12]This transliterated term is almost certainly an item name of foreign origin. Though one could only guess what it is, it may be something like that used to make modern *lokum* desserts. (See footnote on Page 79.)

[13]The use of flour to maintain the form of the poured mixture and prevent sticking is typical in the moulding of sticky *lokum* type confections as it cools.

[14]The "tusk" may be a transcription error incorporated into this edition of *Shuo Fu* 説郛. In the Ming dynasty health and lifestyle compendium, the *Zunsheng Bajian* 遵生八箋, a similar recorded recipe referred to the shape as "elephant eye" instead.[36, Scroll 13] On a separate note, several recipes from the *Wushi Zhongkuilu* were included verbatim in the *Zunsheng Bajian*, which may indicate that the author knows and holds Madame Wu's recipes in high regard.

Madame Wu's Handbook on Home-Cooking

洒孛你方[15]

用熬麼古料熬成,不用核桃。舀上案攤開,用江米末圍定,銅圈印之,即是洒孛你。切象牙者,即名白糖塊。

---

[15] The name "*saboni*" (洒孛你) is almost certainly transliterated from a foreign term. Judging from the name and the method by which this dish was made, it is most likely related to a Turkic confection known as *sabuniye*, which is itself a variant of *lokum*, the chewy sweet commonly known in English as "Turkish delight". The term *sabuniye* means "soap" and is likely named such due to its soap-like translucency or the similarity of its production to the way soap is traditionally made in the Levant (the thick cooked soap is poured onto the floor, spread out, cooled, cut, and lifted out for packaging). The dessert *sabuniye*, or *sabuni*, has appeared in various historical texts. It includes a mention in the travelogue of the 14th-century Moroccan traveller Ibn Battuta [3]. The 19th-century Turkish culinary manual *Melceü't-Tabbâhîn* [14, Altıncı Fasıl:28] provided a recipe for a confection known as *Sabuniye Helvası* made of caramelized sugar, clarified butter, and a cooked starch mixture that was mixed together until it was not sticky. Another confection, known as *sabuniye lokumu*, is still made in areas of Turkey using similar techniques and ingredients as the former. Also, a similarly named confection *sabuni helva/halva-i sabuni*, made with ground almonds, boiled wheat starch, butter, and honey, is still commonly made and enjoyed for its gummy texture. If we assume there are similarities between the *saboni* confection of the Song dynasty version and all of these more modern *sabuniye* and *sabuni*, their recipes could provide hints on the actual composition and full recipe of *saboni*. Perhaps the common elements of these recipes, namely the sugar, butter, and cooked starch mixture, is the *megu* 麼古 simmering mix for *saboni*?

吳氏中饋錄

SHORT PASTRIES

Take four *liang* of butter,[16] one *liang* of honey, one *jin* of white flour, form it together into a dough,[17] pack into a mould to form a cake, and put on the stove.[18] One can substitute lard and use two *liang* of honey instead, also with good results.

酥餅方

油酥四兩,蜜一兩,白麵一斤,搜成劑,入印,作餅,上爐。或用豬油亦可,蜜用二兩,尤好。

---

[16] The original Chinese term used here is *yousu* (油酥), which, according to Dr. Brown, is quite different from the reversed term *suyou* (酥油). While the latter is a dairy product similar to butter or thick clotted cream, the former refers to rendered animal fat. Although this may indicate that animal fat was used for this recipe, the end of this section proposes an alternative recipe using actual rendered animal fat (lard), which may hint that *suyou* may have been reversed in error to *yousu* and that this ingredient was actually a dairy fat such as butter (clarified or otherwise).

[17] The term *souchengji* (搜成劑) translates to "rub into a preparation" or, in modern cooking parlance: "forming/kneading into a dough". The first character "搜" (*sou*), means to "look for" or "search", but in numerous texts up to the early modern period, such as the *Shanjia Qinggong* 山家清供, it was used in conjunction with the character for flour "麵" (*mian*) to indicate rubbing or mixing. The character "劑" (*ji*) is typically used to describe preparations or doses of medication. In the contemporary Song/Yuan dynasty work *Taiping Huimin Hexiaojufang* (太平惠民和劑局方), the fifth scroll contains several traditional Chinese pharmaceutical preparations that use these both *sou* 搜 and *ji* 劑 characters to describe combining and forming various ingredients. It is interesting to note that these two character combinations were used exclusively in these last several recipes.

[18] This is remarkably similar to the way many Western shortbreads are made, though some special apparatus for baking them over the stove is used instead of an oven.

Fried Sandwiched Pastries

Combine the flour mixture into a dough,[19] stuff it with fillings, and sandwich it by folding it over.[20] Pan-fry in oil until done. The filling is the same as that for meat pastries.

油夾兒方

麵搜劑,包餡,作夾兒,油煎熟。餡同肉餅法。

---

[19] There were no indications of what was in this mixture, which could be any combination of fat or water. From this text, it may just be plain dough made of unleavened flour and water.

[20] Such fold-over pastries could well be a relative of the *sanbusak*, which, if true, would put this in the same family tree as everything from the South Asian samosa and Southeast Asian curry puff, to the Caribbean meat patties and Latin American empanadas.

吳氏中饋錄

Little pressed short pastries

Take plain flour and combine together with bean starch. Use one's hands and roll the mixture out into long strings with the diameter of the head of a chopstick. Cut into pieces two *fen* long and mark each one with the patterns on the teeth of a comb.[21] Gather them up, take butter, and fry everything in a pot until done. Ladle them out with a perforated spoon, and while hot, sprinkle with white granulated sugar that has been finely ground, then toss.

酥兒印方

用生麵攙豆粉[22]同和,用手捍成條,如筯頭大,切二分長,逐個用小梳掠印齒花,收起。用酥油,鍋內煠熟,漏杓撈起來,熱筯白砂糖細末,拌之。

---

[21] There are at least three ways to mark a piece of dough with the teeth on a comb: on the side of the comb by pressing and rolling the dough, both perpendicular or parallel to the teeth such that it is marked by parallel lines or using the tip of the teeth and impacting the dough multiple times to get dots. The former two do seem more likely considering they are more straightforward and combs have been used in this manner to mark dough foods in various cultures. As for which of the former two is done if we follow this "principle of straightforwardness." it is likely rolled along the length of the comb, namely, parallel to the teeth if they are long and few, perpendicular to them if they are short and many.

[22] By itself, *doufen* could refer to bean flours such as mung bean starch or soybean flour, although in this case, the former is more likely. The addition of starch to the flour would have made these fried treats more tender and crisper in texture.

Five Fragrance Cakes

Take a combined six *fen* of the best white glutinous rice and *Japonica* rice,[23] take one *fen* of foxnut lily[24] seeds, and one *fen* altogether of ginseng, baizhu[25], fuling,[26] and *sharen*. Grind everything into a fine powder, sieve it, mix it evenly with white granulated sugar cooked in boiling water, and then place it on a steaming vessel.[27]

五香糕方

上白糯米和粳米二、六分,芡實乾一分,人參、白朮、茯苓、砂仁總一分。磨極細,篩過,白沙糖滾湯拌勻,上甑。

---

[23] The *Japonica* variety rice is medium-grained and much stickier than the *Indica* varieties like basmati rice, while being sticky in a different way when compared to the texture of the high amylopectin glutinous rice varieties. These are known quite commonly in colloquial English language as "sushi rice".

[24] The plant *Euryale ferox*, also known as the prickly waterlily.

[25] *Atractylodes macrocephala*, a medicinal plant from the sunflower family

[26] *Wolfiporia extensa*, or rather the large underground sclerotium of the fungus itself. Its outside form and colour resembles a coconut and so does much of its bright white inside with its fine textured flesh.

[27] This recipe is quite similar to a snack known in Taiwanese as "*goh-ah*" (*gaozai*, 糕仔), which is the same mix of ground glutinous and sticky rice powder and other ingredients bound together with boiled sugar syrup and pressed into a mould. Still, a crucial difference exists: the Taiwanese *goh-ah*' are not usually steamed after moulding. Or perhaps this is another version of *songgao* (松糕), which is also quite similar but steamed.

吳氏中饋錄

Boiled sandy balls

Add granulated sugar to azuki bean or mung bean[28] and cook into a large mass. Form into large balls and coat the outside with raw glutinous rice flour. Steam or boil them in liquid.

煮沙團方

砂糖入赤豆或綠豆煮成一團，外以生糯米粉，裹作大團。蒸或滾湯內煮，亦可。

---

[28] The production method of these balls is quite similar to the boiled dessert *yuanxiao* 元宵, which is made by repeatedly coating glutinous rice flour over a ball of sweet filling. Many Han Chinese mistakenly refer to these boiled glutinous desserts as *tangyuan* 湯圓 or "boiled round dumpling", which is understandable since *tangyuan* could be used to collectively refer to any filled or unfilled round glutinous rice balls, respectively wrapped or shaped by hand from the dough. *Yuanxiao* refers explicitly only to filled glutinous rice balls made by rolling sweet filling in flour in the manner described in this recipe. Considering the name of this dessert, the beans may have been coarsely ground or mashed during cooking to give the final product different textures when eaten.

Zongzi

Rinse glutinous rice until clean and fill it with jujubes, chestnuts, dried persimmons, azuki beans, all wrapped in the wild rice stem leaves or the bamboo shoot sheaths.[29] A variation of this involves soaking mugwort leaves with rice. These are known as mugwort fragrance *zongzi*.[30]

粽子法

用糯米淘淨,夾棗、慄、柿乾、銀杏、赤豆,以茭葉或箬葉裹之。一法:以艾葉浸米裹,謂之艾香粽子。

---

[29] Lacking the meaty and savoury ingredients so common in modern Southern Chinese *zongzi*, these Song dynasty ones are decidedly Northern (and dessert) style. These *zongzi* are also likely thinner and smaller in form than the typical modern ones, considering that husks from wild rice stems are used.

[30] *Zongzi* or simply, *zong*, are glutinous rice and fillings wrapped and cooked in a plant-based wrapping, typically the leaves of the broad-leaf bamboo *Indocalamus tessellatus*. Banally referred to in North America as "rice dumpling", or even "Chinese Tamale", *zongzi* are indispensable during Dragon Boat Festival, with different households sharing their family versions of this wrapped food with friends and neighbours during the festivities.

吳氏中饋錄

Jade-filled lung

Take mung bean starch, oil cakes[31], sesame seeds, pine nuts, walnuts, and fennel, mix these six flavours together and roll them up. Put them into the steaming vessel and steam them until done. Cut them into chunks and serve with other foods. It is incredibly delicious. Do not use any oil, add each item, stir together with either starch[32] or flour to steam. It is very good.

玉灌肺方[33]

真粉、油餅、芝麻、松子、胡桃、茴香六味，拌和成捲，入甑蒸熟，切作塊子，供食，美甚。不用油，入各物，粉或麵同拌蒸，亦妙。

---

[31] These were most likely broken crumbs from various oily flatbreads analogous to modern *youbing* 油餅. This usage of old stale starch food would make it quite similar to how old bread in the West is shredded into bread crumbs and used as a filler or how the left-over bits from frying tempura (*tenkatsu* 天かす) are added to other Japanese dishes to give a crunchy texture. The mention of "oil cakes" as an ingredient here may also hint at how common these oily flatbreads were during the Song dynasty, enough for their crumbs or stale specimens to be used in their own right.

[32] The character *fen* 粉 here could refer to rice flour or any other starch, but considering this recipe, either is probably fine.

[33] A very similar recipe for this dish was also given in the *Shanjia Qinggong* (山家清供):「真粉、油饼、芝蔴、松子、核桃去皮，加莳萝少许，白糖红曲少许，为末拌和，入甑蒸熟，切作肺样块子，用辣汁供。」Whether this was duplication or which was the original source, is unclear. Regardless, the instructions in this recipe seems be all over the place and does leave one rather confused.

Wontons

Take one *jin* of white flour, three *qian* of salt, in the manner of hanging *suo* noodles[34]. Add more water occasionally when mixing and form it into dough for making noodles. After some time,[35] knead the mixture a hundred times, then pull it into small pieces. Spread them out and use mung bean starch in the manner of powdered rice bran,[36] All four sides should be made thin, put in the filling, and secure the wrapper.[37].

餛飩方

白麵一斤、鹽三錢和,如落索麵,更頻入水搜,和為餅劑。
少頃,操百遍,捌為小塊,捍開,菉豆粉為椊,四邊要薄,
入餡,其皮堅。

---

[34] *Suo* noodles (*soumian*, 索麵) or "rope noodles" are a type of noodle produced by pulling them, then wrapping and stretching them around a pair of sticks until they are 1-2 mm in diameter. These are the predecessors of modern "longevity noodles" (*changshoumian*, 長壽麵), *su* noodles (*sumian*, 素麵), and Japanese *somen* 素麵.

[35] Let the dough rest before kneading. In bread making, this would be typically around twenty to thirty minutes.

[36] Rice bran is used in many Chinese culinary applications, from cleaning animal innards before cooking, to a bulking agent for fermenting foods, and as we find out here, it was also used as a coating to prevent pastries from sticking together. The fact that this was explicitly mentioned may hint that it was not standard practice at the time to use starch to prevent food from sticking, and using bran to do so was more typical.

[37] This means that each wonton must be well-sealed so it does not open up and spill its filling when cooked.

吳氏中饋錄

Slippery water noodles

Use the whitest flour,[38] knead, and form into a unit of dough. From each *jin*, make many dozen pieces.[39] Place them in water, and let them rise until quite large.[40] Pull and draw out each piece and put into boiling water until done. The thinner and broader one draws it the better.[41] Top with sesame paste, apricot kernel paste, salted dried bamboo shoot, soy pickled cucumbers, lees pickled eggplants, ginger, salt pickled garlic chives, and shredded cucumbers. One can also add pan-fried meat to make it truly wonderful.[42]

水滑麵方

用十分白麵,揉搜成劑。一斤作十數塊,放在水內,候其麵性發得十分滿足,逐塊抽、拽下湯煮熟,抽、拽得闊薄乃好。麻膩、杏仁膩、醎笋乾、醬瓜、糟茄、姜薑、醃韭、黃瓜絲作虀頭,或加煎肉,尤妙。

---

[38] The term *shifen* 十分 could also translate to "ten *fen*" (the unit equivalent to $\frac{1}{100}^{th}$ of a *liang*). However, this is unlikely since this quantity would indicate making a tiny quantity of dough with around 4g of flour.

[39] *Shishukui* (十數塊) translates literally to "many tens of pieces". However, this phrase is awkward in English and thus the equivalent "many dozen pieces" is used here instead.

[40] Using leavened dough for noodle making is less common but still found in specialty Chinese restaurants and food stalls that specialize in them. The texture of such noodles is surprisingly smooth and light.

[41] This pulling technique seems similar to the technique for *biang biang* noodles and sash noodles (褲帶麵, *kudai mian*).

[42] These boiled noodles, served with sesame paste and savoury dry toppings like this, would be in the right place served at modern street food stalls all over East Asia.

THIN SUGAR CRISPS

Take one *jin* and four *liang* of white sugar, one *jin* and four *liang* of clear oil, two bowls of water, five *jin* of white flour, adding a small amount of butter and Sichuan pepper, salt, and water. Form together into dough, roll flat into a disk the size of a *jiu* jar's opening.[43] Sprinkle their tops evenly with dehulled sesame and bake them in the oven until done. They are fragrant and aromatic to eat.

糖薄脆法

白糖一斤四兩,清油一斤四兩,水二碗,白麵五斤,加酥油、椒鹽、水少許。搜和成劑,捍薄,如酒鍾口大,上用去皮芝麻撒勻,入爐燒熟,食之香脆。

---

[43] The size of the opening is variable depending on the size of the jar used for the beverage, but 10-15cm would be most common.

吳氏中饋錄

Sugar torreya

Add white flour to the dough starter and let rise. Add boiling water and form into a dough. Cut it into the shape of torreya nuts[44] and put them into boiling hot oil to fry. Wrap them in sugar dough, where this wrapping mixture is sugar and flour in equal proportions formed into a dough.

糖榧方

白麵入酵待發,滾湯搜成劑,切作榧子樣,下十分滾油煠過取出,糖麵內纏之,其纏糖與麵對和成劑。

---

[44]The edible drupe kernels of the tree *Torreya nucifera*.

GLOSSARY

Black cardamom (*caoguo,* 草果) A spice with large, brown, finely ridged pods from the dried fruits of *Amomum tsao-ko*. These cardamom pods are larger and have a slightly sweeter fragrance than that of the green cardamom (*Amomum subulatum*) commonly found in Western supermarkets. Seldom used in modern Chinese cuisines, this book's medieval Chinese recipes often featured black cardamom in a mix of other spices.

***Douchi* 豆豉** This ingredient is a dry, dark-coloured and sharp-flavoured fermented soybean product. Commonly known in English as "fermented black bean" due to its outward appearance, it is the oldest known fermented soy ingredient still commonly used in Chinese cuisine. *Douchi* is made by cultivating soaked and steamed soybeans with the spores of *Aspergillus oryzae* or *Aspergillus sojae* (*qujun,* 麴菌), then pickling them with salt, and then drying them.

Douchi is also considered the direct predecessors of fermented Chinese soy pastes and soy-sauces since they are all based on the same cultured soybean ingredient, known in this book as *huangzi* 黃子 (See Page 97). Indeed, the fact that Taiwanese soy-sauce (*yinyou,* 蔭油) is made by aged, undried douchi, and the Cantonese name for soy-sauce is *si-*

yau 豉油, points to this connection. Although it plays a less prominent culinary role nowadays than soy-sauce or even soy paste, it is still a key ingredient in many dishes, such as the well-loved "douchi stir-fried with clams" (*chizhi chaoxian*, 豉汁炒蜆) or the ubiquitous "steamed black bean spareribs" (*chizhi paigu*, 豉汁排骨) found on the menus of dim-sum restaurants worldwide.

Fen 粉 Usually translated as "powder" in daily context, the word *fen* has additional meanings in Chinese cuisine and is used to refer to:

- **Raw plant starches:** Sweet potato starch is referred to as *fanshu fen*, 番薯粉 and tapioca is *mushu fen* 木薯粉. The Chinese term for starch itself is *dian fen* 澱粉, which translates to "sedimented powder", perfectly describing how starch is collected and processed from raw plant material.

- **Various grain-flours:** Wheat flour (*mian fen*, 麵粉) or rice flour (*mi fen*, 米粉) are just two examples *fen* used to describe grain flours. However, one should note that wheat flour is never directly referred to as *fen*, even when the context is known (See *Mian* on Page 94 for a discussion on wheat flour).

- **Starch-based noodles:** Mung-bean vermicelli is known as *dongfen* 冬粉, and sweet potato noodles are *fanshu fen* 番薯粉 are two common examples of this. Sometimes, the names of starch noodles are combined with a word describing its shape or form, such as *fensi* 粉絲 (*lit.* starch floss) or *fentiao* 粉條 (*lit.* starch strips), to help disambiguate the noodles from the raw starches.

- **Rice-based noodles:** For example, rice vermicelli are *mifen* 米粉 and rice noodles rolls are *changfen* 腸粉 (*lit.* sausage/intestine starch).

- **Various other powdered ingredients:** For example, chili powder is known as *lajiao fen* 辣椒粉 and powdered sugar is called *tang fen* 糖粉, as well as all manners of ground spices.

When the context is believed to be understood, all disambiguating characters for the *fen*-containing terms are often omitted for the sake of brevity. Even in modern times, this ambiguity can lead to culinary miscommunications, especially when the dish is unfamiliar to the cook. Years ago, I met somebody who tried following a recipe for making Italian polenta from a Chinese language cookbook but failed in her first attempt for this exact reason. Instead of using the expected corn flour or corn meal (*yumi fen*, 玉米粉), she used corn starch (*yumi fen*, 玉米粉) to prepare the food, with rather different results. One cannot help but wonder how many such mistakes we unintentionally make while reading old, arguably foreign, recipes like the ones in this book.

Fragrant oil The term "fragrant oil" (*xiangyou*, 香油) is used in modern times as well as centuries passed to refer to sesame oil. To confer it such a name, people during the Song dynasty, as in now, were clearly entranced by the aromas of the oil expressed from roasted sesame seeds (*Sesamum indicum*). However, it is not always clear from reading the text whether the term refers to sesame oil or another particularly fragrant oil or whether its usage has shifted over time. Thus, we translate this term literally whenever it appears in the original Chinese text, even if we are reasonably confident that it is sesame oil.

Jiu (酒) A Mandarin word used to describe all manners of alcoholic beverages, be they brewed, distilled, or concocted. While the character "酒" itself was used in the Chinese languages to describe brewed rice or millet-based alcoholic drinks since its inception in Bronze Age China, with centuries and millennia of continuous agricultural, technological, and cultural development, it has broadened to refer to most ethanol solutions or mixtures, regardless of whether they are consumable or not.

Although *jiu* was traditionally translated into English and other Western languages as "wine", this is technically inaccurate because of how Chinese *jiu* is fermented from starchy grains rather than sugary fruit. Furthermore, referring to it as "wine" would effectively exclude all other alcoholic beverages referred to by this word, whether they are Western cocktails (*jiwei jiu*, 雞尾酒) or the traditional distilled *baijiu* 白酒. Other translation choices bantered about in academia or by enthusiasts, such as the wordy "Chinese alcoholic beverages", also failed to capture the context of this word accurately. Due to the lack of satisfactory translations, we have chosen to use the Mandarin transliteration directly, as is, in this book. For those who require a more thorough, or perhaps drawn-out, discussion of our reasoning for using "*jiu*", please refer to the "A Note on *Jiu* 酒" section in *Recipes from the Garden of Contentment* [8, p.xxxii], which is still quite relevant to this conversation.

Jiu-lees In this book, we use *jiu*-lees to refer to the lees remaining after the fermented alcoholic *jiu* 酒 was pressed out after brewing. Know simply as *zao* 糟 in Chinese, the lees from the traditional *jiu* production would have mainly consisted of leftover yeast and fibre from the fermented grain, typically rice. The sticky mass would still contain a lot of enzymatic and biological activity, as well as flavour compounds from the brewing process, which could be used to preserve, pickle, or flavour other food items. Across East Asia, this ingredient is still commonly used for cuisine in regions with thriving brewing industries. However, with the decline in home pickling and preservation, much of the produced *jiu*-lees are now fed to livestock animals as nutritive supplements mixed into their feed.

Mian (麵) A word that is used most commonly refers almost exclusively to wheat-based foods and ingredients such as wheat dough (*mianfen*, 麵糰), wheat flour (*mianfen*, 麵粉), and wheat-based noodles or pasta (*miantiao*, 麵條). However, it is also used to refer to powders colloquially. For instance, chilli powder or powder mixtures in some regions of China are known as "*lajiao mian*" 辣椒麵 rather than the more typical way of referring to it: "*lajiao fen*" 辣椒粉. When the context is believed to be understood, disambiguating characters for the *mian*-containing terms will often be omitted, which inside more unfamiliar or poorly written recipes would force one to hazard guesses on whether wheat dough, flour, or noodle was supposed to be used as ingredients.

Qing (青) Typically translated as "blue-green", *qing* is one of those cultural colour words [5] that existed since the early history of China. Archaic forms of the character "青" were found in proclamation texts inscribed during the Western Zhou period (1045 BCE – 771 BCE) cast onto the ceremonial bronze vessels of that time. Throughout history, the word was used to describe a swath of hues ranging from the bright greens, blues, and indigos to the glossy greys and blacks [20]. Although mostly superseded by more specific colour names in modern Chinese, the word is still commonly used, especially for artistic expression or when attempting to evoke feelings of tradition.

In terms of translation, the fact that *qing* maps to multiple English colour words means that each instance of its use needs to be resolved separately using the context and cues from surrounding text. For instance, when used to describe the colour of gourds or cucumbers, we translated the word as "green" (See Page 34), but when used in the name of an ingredient such as *qing yu* 青魚, we translated the whole name as "black carp" (See Page 12).

On the character's etymology, we see in its earliest forms that *qing* 青 was actually vertically composed of the character for "birth/growth" (*sheng*, 生) and interestingly, another archaic colour character: "reddish" (*dan*, 丹). Sadly, the actual meaning behind this combination of characters is lost.

Qu **(麴)** A word for any manner of grains cultured with domesticated species of microorganisms and used as a fermentation starter for producing various fermented seasonings or drinks. Chinese alcoholic beverages (*jiu*), vinegar, and fermented soy foods are all rooted in the use of *qu* starter; thus, its successful production using raw grain is paramount. A bad or contaminated batch of *qu* could potentially ruin a manufacturer of the fermented or brewed products, and thus, the task of producing them is left to only the most highly skilled artisans.

Most *qu* do not consist of a mono-culture of one microorganism but are made up of a complex colony of bacteria, yeast, and mould, all bred together and harmonized over centuries of continuous production. The grains used also differ depending on the geographic region and climate, with rice, wheat, and sorghum commonly used. Due to the complex mixtures of microorganisms and grain used in different *qu*, the flavours of the fermented products made from them are correspondingly unique. These unassuming chunks of cultured grains could be considered a living cultural treasure of Chinese gastronomy since we would have lost the very core of Chinese cuisine without them.

Red ferment starter Know in Chinese as *hongqu* 紅曲/紅麴 and commonly known in English as "red yeast rice", this starter culture is made by cultivating *Monascus purpureus* or *Monascus ruber* on long grain rice. The grains of this starter are dark reddish purple and stain everything prepared with it in a striking vermillion colour. They could be directly used in cooking, combined with other cooked grains to ferment them into a bright red seasoning paste, or used in conjunction with other starters to ferment other food or drink.

Sharen (砂仁) / Susha (宿砂) The mature dried fruits of the plant *Amomum villosum var. xanthioides* consisting of brown, spiky, ridged, rough-textured pods. They are sometimes called "large cardamom", though confusingly this same term is also sometimes used to refer to black cardamom. Their name is also written as "縮砂" (*susha*), and quite commonly referred to as "縮砂仁" (*susha ren*), the latter referring specifically to the fragrant seeds that are sold pre-shelled from the dried pods.

Yellow grain There are several references to "yellow grains" (*huangzi*, 黃子) in the text, though this text also provided no clear definitions for what exactly they are. However, an educated guess would be that the most likely candidate for it is a type of *qu* 麴, consisting of *Aspergillus oryzae* or *Aspergillus sojae* cultured legume and grain (See *qu* on Page 96), similar to that used to make fermented soy paste or *douchi* (See Page 91). Indeed, in the "Compendium of Materia Medica" (*Bencao Gangmu*, 本草綱目), the author Li Shizhen 李時珍 noted that the "women's grain starter" (*nuqu*, 女麴), cultivated on wheat grain, was also known as "yellow grain".

Considering that the colour of *Aspergillus* spores for this type of *qu* starter is always a yellow-green hue regardless of the type of grain used, *qu* growing on soybeans would still fit the term. Looking at the later recipes for making *douchi* (See "Water *douchi*" on Page 69) and fermented vegetables (See "Making *jiu douchi*" on Page 68), leads one to believe that yellow grain is likely soybeans and wheat cultured with yellowish *qu*, known as *doupu* (written variously as 豆蒲, 豆脯, or even 豆譜). The recipe for Pickled yellow sparrows (See Page 23) used a type of cultured wheat grain, known as "yellowed wheat" (*maihuang*, 麥黃), which was most likely related to yellow grain.

Ume These are the small, intensely sour and astringent fruits of the East Asian apricot (*Prunus mume*), which are used to make

吳氏中饋錄

a wide range of pickled and preserved foods throughout the region. Although a loanword of Japanese origin, *ume* 梅 has quickly become more commonly used in English in recent years to reference the fruit of this beloved tree, compared to Mandarin name: "*mei*" 梅, hence we use for the translated text. It is also a far more precise term when compared to the erroneous but all too commonly used translation in English, "plum" or "Chinese plum". The distinct spelling of *ume* is also concise and unambiguous, which makes it much preferred over the awkward but technically accurate English name "flowering apricot".

Wild rice stem Known as *jiaobai* 茭白 in Chinese, wild rice stem is the thickened inner sheaths of the East Asian aquatic grass *Zizania latifolia* that has been infected by the fungus *Ustilago esculenta* (closely related to the corn smut fungus). After being harvested from its shallow ponds and the thick sheaths of the stem had been peeled like bamboo shoots, a firm creamy-white plump center "shoot" is revealed. When stir-fried, this shoot-like food is delectably crisp in texture, refreshingly sweet, and utterly delicious. The cultivation of this vegetable is restricted in North America for fear that the fungus will jump from its cultivated host to the genetically similar to the American wild rice *Zizania palustris*.

BIBLIOGRAPHY

[1] ANDERSON, E. N., WANG, T., AND MAIR, V. H. *69. Ni Zan, Cloud Forest Hall Collection of Rules for Drinking and Eating.* University of Hawaii Press, Honolulu, 2005, pp. 444–455.

[2] ATWOOD, C. The textual history of Tao Zongyi's Shuofu: Preliminary results of stemmatic research on the Shengwu Qinzheng Lu. *Sino-Platonic Papetrs, 271* (06 2017).

[3] BATTUTA, I. *The Rihla, or A Masterpiece to Those Who Contemplate the Wonders of Cities and the Marvels of Travelling.* Morocco, 1355.

[4] BEDINI, S. *The Scent of Time: A Study of the Use of Fire and Incense for Time Measurement in Oriental Countries.* American Philosophical Soc.: Transactions of the ... . New series. American Philosophical Society, 1963.

[5] BERLIN, B., AND KAY, P. *Basic Color Terms: their Universality and Evolution.* University of California Press, Berkeley and Los Angeles, 1969.

[6] BUELL, P. D., AND ANDERSON, E. N. *A Soup for the Qan: Chinese Dietary Medicine of the Mongol Era As Seen in Hu Sihui's Yinshan Zhengyao: Introduction, Translation, Commentary, and Chinese Text. Second Revised and Expanded Edition.* Brill, Leiden, The Netherlands, 2010.

[7] BUELL, P. D., ANDERSON, E. N., DE PABLO MOYA, M., AND OSKENBAY, M. *Crossroads of Cuisine: The Eurasian Heartland, the Silk Roads and Food*. Brill, Leiden, The Netherlands, 2020.

[8] CHEN, S. J.-S., AND YUAN, M. *Recipes from the Garden of Contentment: Yuan Mei's Manual of Gastronomy*. Berkshire Publishing Group, 2018.

[9] FAN, S.-C., AND SHENG-HAN, S. *On "Fan Shengzhi Shu,": An Agriculturistic Book of China Written in the First Century B.C.* Science Press, 1963.

[10] FENG, J. The female chef and the nation: Zeng Yi's "Zhongkui lu" (records from the kitchen). *Modern Chinese Literature and Culture 28*, 1 (2016), 1–37.

[11] FREEMAN, M. Sung. In *Food in Chinese Culture: Anthropological and Historical Perspectives*, K. C. Chang, Ed., A Yale paperbound. Yale University Press, 1977, pp. 141–176.

[12] GOODY, J. *Cooking, Cuisine and Class: A Study in Comparative Sociology*. Themes in the Social Sciences. Cambridge University Press, 1982.

[13] HUANG, H. *Biology and Biological Technology. Part 5: Fermentations and Food Science*, vol. 6 of *Science and Civilisation in China*. Cambridge University Press, 2000.

[14] KÂMIL, M. *Melceü't-Tabbâhîn*. Ottoman Empire, 1844.

[15] LIN, H.-J., AND LIN, T. *Chinese Gastronomy*. Hastings House, 1969.

[16] NEEDHAM, J., AND BRAY, F. *Science and Civilisation in China, Part 2, Agriculture*. Science and Civilisation in China. Cambridge University Press, 1984.

[17] OTSUKA, H. Soy sauce in the chinese language. *Journal of the Kikkoman Institute for International Food Culture, 21* (7 2021), 3–8.

[18] PHILLIPS, C. *All Under Heaven: Recipes from the 35 Cuisines of China*. McSweeney's/Ten Speed Press, 2016.

[19] TORA, Y. Weights and measures. In *Salt Production Techniques in Ancient China*. Brill, 1992, pp. xi–xvi.

[20] WANG, H. A Bias of Frequency: Qing as a Composite Category in Mandarin. 2022/01/13 Universität Heidelberg, Heidelberg, Germany, 01 2022.

[21] XI, L. Cookbook writing and the women in the late qing: A study on Zeng Yi's Zhong Kui Lu — "食书" 书写与晚清女性：以曾懿《中馈录》为中心的研究. College of History, Nankai University, Tianjin, 300350, China, 2017.

[22] XI, L. [奚丽芳] 食与色：食谱与中国性别史研究. 中国史研究动态 (3 2023).

[23] 元著 [YUAN DYNASTY AUTHORS]. 居家必用事类全集 *[Jujiabiyoung Shilei Quanji]*. 元 [Yuan], 1279–1368.

[24] 方以智 [FANG YIZHI]. 物理小識 *[Wuli Xiaoshi]*. 明 [Ming].

[25] 易 [AUTHORS OF THE YIJING]. 易經 *[Yi Jing]*. 西周 [Western Zhou], 800 BCE.

[26] 李勣 [LI JI], AND 蘇敬奏 [SU JINGZOU]. 唐本草 *[Tang Bencao]* / 新修本草 *[Xinxiu Bencao]*. 唐 [Tang], 739.

[27] 李昉 [LI FANG]. 太平御覽 *[Taiping Yulan]*. 宋 [Song].

[28] 李時珍 [LI SHIZHEN]. 本草綱目 *[Bencao Gangmu]*. 金陵 [Jinling, modern day Nanjing 南京], 1596.

[29] 林洪 [LIN HONG]. 山家清供 *[Shanjia Qinggong]*. 泉州 [Quanzhou city], 南宋 [Southern Song], 1127-1279.

[30] 蘭陵笑笑生 [LANLING XIAOXIAOSHENG]. 金瓶梅 *[Jinpingmei]*. 明 [Ming], 1610.

[31] 賈思勰 [JIA SIXIE]. 齊民要術 *[Qimin Yaoshu]*. 東魏 [Northern Wei], 544.

吳氏中饋錄

[32] 釋贊寧 [Shi Zanning]. 筍譜 *[Sunpu]*. 宋 [Song].

[33] 陳承 [Chen Cheng]. 太平惠民和劑局方 *[Taipinghuimin Hejijufang]*. 宋 [Song].

[34] 陳藏器 [Chen Cangqi]. 本草拾遺 *[Bencao Shiyi]*. 唐 [Tang], 739.

[35] 陶宗儀 [Tao Zongyi]. 說郛 *[Shuofu]*. 元 [Yuan], 1400s.

[36] 高濂 [Gao Lian]. 遵生八箋 *[Zunshengbajian]*. 明 [Ming], 1591.

INDEX

Alum, 35, 60, 70
Apricot kernel, 31, 54, 69
    paste, 88
Arabic, 8
Ash
    Alkaline solution, 26
    Stone, 64
        See also Slaked lime
    Wood, 24
Autumn, 16, 35, 43

Bailian (*Ampelopsis japonica*), 27
Baizhi (*Angelica dahurica*), 45
Baizhu (*Atractylodes macrocephala*), 83
Baking, 9, 89
Bamboo
    Dried shoots, 7, 88
    Leaves, 4, 5
    Shoot sheaths, 23, 31, 85
    Shoots, 24, 66, 67
    Slats, 23, 31, 68
Bean

吳氏中饋錄

Azuki bean, 26, 54, 84, 85
Mung bean, 26, 84
   Starch, 82, 86, 87
Soy bean, 31, 62, 70
   Sprouts, 52
Bencao Gangmu, 23, 70, 97
Bencao Shiyi, 64
Black cardamom, 3, 6, 13, 69
Boiling, 6, 9, 15, 20, 31, 36, 45, 49, 84
   Brine, 67
   Water, 25, 39, 46, 47, 52–54, 59, 60, 64, 67, 69, 83, 88, 90
Brassica (Plant Genus), 39, 46, 62
Broad-leaf bamboo (*Indocalamus tessellatus*), 4, 85

Cassia, 69
Central Asia, 77
Chicken, 7, 9
Chinese honey locust (*Gleditsia sinensis*), 24
Chishi Shijing, xxiii
Citron (*Citrus medica*), 40
Clam, 21
   Razor, 17
Copper as colorant and preservative, 57
Costus (*Saussurea costus*), 69
Crab, 3, 18, 21, 24, 26
Cucumber
   Fresh, 26, 34–36, 50, 68, 88
   Pickled, 7, 13, 88
   See also Gourd

Dill, 53, 54, 58
Divine starter, 14
Douchi, 68, 69, 97
Drying, 35
   Air, 47, 54, 55, 58, 60, 61
   Drip, 33

Hot tile, 49
Press, 11, 49
Shade, 37
Simmer, 70
Sun, 8, 19, 33, 34, 36, 38, 42–44, 53–55, 59, 62, 68, 70
Wind, 5, 12, 31, 37, 44, 64, 67
Wring, 6, 46, 52, 59, 66

East Asia, xiv, xvii, 39, 97
Eggplant, 26, 31, 33, 35, 41, 49, 54–57, 59, 68, 88
Eurasian siskin (*Spinus spinus*), 23

Fat, 77
    Butter, 76, 80, 82, 89
    Lard, 80
Fennel, 3, 12, 14, 22, 31, 33, 34, 46, 47, 51, 54, 58, 68, 69, 86
Fish, 14
    Black carp, 12
    Carp, 5
    Grenadier Anchovies, 4
    Preparation strategies, 20, 24
    Pressed, 17
    Shad, 10
Fish sauce, 14
Flour
    Glutinous rice, 84
    Rice, 78
    Toasted Wheat, 77
    Wheat, 24, 75, 76, 80–82, 86
    White wheat, 87–90
Foxnut lily (*Euryale ferox*), 83
Frying, 54, 81, 82, 90
Fuling (*Wolfiporia extensa*), 83

Garlic, 13, 35, 37, 44, 48, 60, 72
Garlic chives, 61, 88

吳氏中饋錄

Ginger, 3, 7, 14, 17, 31, 34, 43, 46, 47, 59, 62, 68, 69, 88
Gourd, 31, 34, 59
Green onion, 3, 14
    Chopped, 47
    Slivers, 17, 23, 58
    Whites, 7, 22

Honey, 80

Japanese Quail (*Coturnix japonica*), 54
Jiu (Alcoholic Beverage), 9, 10, 14, 17, 18, 22, 23, 26, 31, 35, 45, 68, 69
    Good quality, 16
Jiu-lees, 5, 15, 18, 26, 41–43, 57

Licorice, 31, 36, 45, 54
    Extract, 44
Lokum, 78, 79
Loquat seeds, 21
Lotus shoots, 58

Mandarin peel, 13, 17, 22, 31, 34, 40, 46, 47, 53, 54, 68, 69
Mandarine, 26
Meat sauce, 22
Mint, 24, 33, 34
Monascus (Mold Genus), 14, 23, 47, 58
Musculus senhousei (Shellfish species), 21
Mutton, 6

Napa cabbage, 63
    See also Brassica (Plant Genus)
Noodles, 25, 87, 88

Pan-fry, 81, 88
Parmelia saxatilis (Lichin species), 40
Pepper (*Piper nigrum*), 3
Perilla

Leaves, 34, 36, 59
Whole, 31
Pine
Needles, 26
Nuts, 86
Pork, 6, 8, 11, 13, 24, 25
Preparation strategies, 11, 18–21, 24

Qimin Yaoshu, iii, 14, 26, 70

Radish, 42
Pickled, 13
White, 47
Raw
Crab, 3
Pork, 13
Red algae (*Gelidium amansii*), 40
Rice, 53
Bran, 87
Cooked, 17
Flour, 78, 86
Glutinous, 83, 85
flour, 84
Ground, 17
Japonica, 83

Salt, 3, 5, 6, 9, 12, 16–19, 23, 24, 31, 33–38, 41, 42, 44–47, 50, 51, 53, 55, 57–62, 64, 69, 70, 72, 87–89
Brine, 51, 55, 62, 64, 67, 69, 72
Good quality, 69
Ground, 22, 54
Hot, 11
Toasted, 5, 12, 14, 48, 68
Sappanwood (*Biancaea sappan*), 70
Sesame
Fragrant oil, 7, 13, 18, 54, 61

吳氏中饋錄

Oil, 3, 52
Paste, 88
Seeds, 86, 89
Shanjia Qinggong, 80, 86
Sharen, 3, 6, 8, 10, 13, 31, 34, 83
Shrimp, 16, 19
    Dried, 7, 19
Sichuan pepper, 10, 12–14, 16, 22, 23, 31, 51–54, 58, 69, 89
    Green, 68
    Ground, 3, 8, 47
    Oil, 6
Slaked lime, 35, 60
    See also Ash: Stone
South Asia, 81
Southeast Asia, 14, 76, 77, 81
Soy-paste, 7, 10, 22, 26, 34, 36, 37, 40, 53, 54, 97
Soy-sauce, 13, 18, 52
Star anise, 46, 47, 69
Steaming, 8, 10, 33, 36, 37, 44, 53, 54, 66, 83, 84, 86
Stir-fry, 7, 9, 13, 19, 34, 46, 62
Sugar, 37, 59, 90
    Granulated, 8, 24, 33, 34, 53, 82, 84
    Powder, 77
    Syrup, 76
    White, 52, 77, 83, 89

Taiping Yulan, 34
Tang Bencao, 64

Ume (*Prunus mume*), 70, 72

Vegetal soap, 24
Vinegar, 3, 6, 9, 13, 18, 25, 33, 35, 46, 48, 52, 53, 59
    Good quality, 60
    Mild, 39, 45

Walnut, 78, 86

Wild rice stem (*jiaobai*), 7, 47, 58
    Leaves, 85

Yellow breasted bunting (*Emberiza aureola*), 23
Yellow grain, 50, 68, 69

Zongzi, 85

www.ingramcontent.com/pod-product-compliance
Lightning Source LLC
Chambersburg PA
CBHW061148170426
43209CB00012B/1596